NO GLORY WITHOUT A STORY!

Stepping out on Faith to Birth the Business within You!

Edited & Organized by
Dr. Mia Y. Merritt

ISBN: 978-1-63752-980-5

NO GLORY WITHOUT A STORY!
Written by: a collection of authors
Published by Merritt Publishing Company

Library of Congress Cataloging
in-Publication Data

First Printing 2021
Printed in the U.S.A.

Genre Category:
Self-help, inspiration, business, motivation, spirituality, Christianity,
personal development, confidence building, young adult

Dedication

This book is dedicated to all of the entrepreneurs out there waiting to be born.

Many aspiring entrepreneurs struggle with believing that they are good enough to start a business and be successful at it. This book is dedicated to those of you who have been dreaming about starting your own business, but for whatever reason, you have not yet done it. Fear, uncertainty, self-doubt, or fear of failure may be preventing you from moving forward. Know that those are normal feelings that people experience when they consider the idea of starting their own businesses, but you will never know what you could accomplish or how successful you can be if you don't pursue your dreams. Starting a business does not have to be an all or nothing situation. Some of the best businesses are started while people are still working full-time jobs, as you will discover through some of the stories in this book. It is the desire of each author in this book that, after reading their stories, you will be motivated to put your passion to work and step out on faith to bring into fruition, the gift of entrepreneurship that is already in you!

About the Organizer

 Mia Y. Merritt, Ed.D, was born and raised in Miami, Florida and attended the Miami-Dade County Public School System. She is an educator with over 27 years' experience serving as a teacher, administrator, university professor, subject matter expert and educational consultant. She is a Certified Keynote Speaker, Teen/Youth Facilitator, prolific author and ordained minister.

"No Glory Without a Story" (NGWS) is a series of books that Dr. Merritt has organized with various authors. Each edition has a different focus. Outside of the NGWS series, Dr. Merritt has published 17 books on the subjects of spirituality, personal development, prosperity, self-empowerment, and adult education. She is the CEO of Merritt Publishing Company and Merritt Consulting, Inc., which provides services in educational programs, curriculum development, corporate retreats, conference speaking, seminars, staff development and teen/youth training.

Dr. Merritt is also a recipient of the African American Achiever's Award sponsored by JM Family Enterprises, recognized by Legacy Magazine as one of South Florida's 25 Most Influential & Prominent Black Women in Business and Leadership, and Phi Delta Kappa Educator of the Year. Dr. Merritt is a graduate of Leadership Broward, Class 33 and holds memberships in many community organizations and professional boards. She has a Doctorate Degree in Organizational Leadership, a Masters Degree in Exceptional Education, a Masters Degree in Psychology, a Specialist Degree in Educational Leadership and a Bachelors Degree in Elementary Education.

Introduction

In a perfect world, we all would have unlimited capital to fund our dream businesses. Unfortunately, that is not our reality. Most of us have to be a little creative when it comes to finding the funds needed to start a business. Many people take out business loans, deplete their savings, borrow from retirement accounts, cash in policies or liquidate stocks in order to get the funds needed to get started. However, if you are confident that there is a need for your business, that your products or services appeal to the right market and you already have a unique selling proposition that sets you apart from the competition, then don't let anything deter you from pursuing your dream. The authors of this book stepped out on faith to pursue their dreams of becoming entrepreneurs and they have reaped the benefits of their faith. In this book, they share stories of what precipitated their first steps of faith towards starting their businesses and they talk about the good, the bad, the successes and the failures. It is my desire that their stories will inspire, motivate and ignite a fire in you which will propel you to take that leap of faith!

Dr. Mia Y. Merritt

Table of Contents

NO GLORY WITHOUT A STORY!

*Stepping out on Faith to Birth the
Business within You!*

3rd Edition

About the Author
Dr. Barbara M. Sharief

Dr. Barbara Sharief wears many hats and balances them all quite well. She is currently a County Commissioner in Broward County, Florida and also the Founder/CEO of South Florida Pediatric Homecare. Dr. Sharief was born in South Florida, raised in Miami and is a long-time resident of Broward County. She is a mother of three daughters Amanda, Alyssa and Hailey, and has always made the time to be an active volunteer in their Schools.

Dr. Sharief has a Doctorate Degree of Nursing Practice, a Masters of Science Degree in Nursing, a Bachelor of Science in Nursing, and an Advanced Registered Nurse Practitioner Degree. She has more than 28 years experience in the specialized field of issues pertaining to medically complex children. In 2001, Dr. Sharief founded South Florida Pediatric Homecare Inc. The company serves residents of Broward and Miami-Dade Counties providing jobs for approximately 200 professionals in South Florida. The company is considered one of the top home health care agencies in Broward and Miami-Dade Counties for the care of children and adults with complex medical issues. Dr. Sharief's commitment to her community led her to public service through politics.

Dr. Sharief was Commissioner and Vice-Mayor for the City of Miramar from 2009 to 2010. In 2010, she was elected to the Broward County Commission, District 8, which serves a culturally diverse population. In 2013, she was selected as the first African American Mayor of Broward County and in 2016, was selected once again as Broward County's Mayor. Dr. Sharief is a member of many organizations, holds leadership positions, and has received a plethora of awards and recognitions. As of the printing of this book (2021), Dr. Sharief was running for U.S. Congress in Florida District 20 to continue to advocate for others.

Chapter 1

Pursuing my Dream of Starting my Business:
From Vision to Victory!

Dr. Barbara Sharief

President/CEO South Florida Pediatric Homecare Inc.

People often ask me where my inspiration to be a business owner came from? As a child growing up in Miami, Florida, I followed my entrepreneurial father around as he developed his clothing store business. He was focused, determined and very driven to succeed in order to care for his wife and eight children. He had no more than a ninth-grade education, yet he achieved what many with college degrees only dreamed of. In my family, there was always a strong emphasis placed on education. My father, James Muhammad Sharief, would never expect anything less than me finishing college and being successful in life. He would always say *"You better stay in school and get your degree. Remember, people can take a lot of things from you, but once you get that knowledge, it is yours, and that knowledge stays with you forever"*. I remember asking my dad, *"If getting college papers was so important then where is yours?"* That is when he told me that he never graduated from college and he only finished the ninth grade. He started working at such a young age, that he never had the opportunity to finish high school or go to college. Dad said that he wanted the best for me, and that I had to do better than him to make him proud.

Watching my father negotiate the price of clothes with manufacturers really piqued my interest in business. I learned that the less he paid for a garment, the better his profit was when he sold it. Pretty basic stuff, but he started selling clothes out of a dodge box truck. We would sit in front of a restaurant called Jumbo's Seafood all day and night selling the clothes. My mother would bring us dinner and it seemed that the days were never ending. My father would try to send me home, but I would not budge. I found his business exciting and I felt (at that age) like I was his assistant. When people would come up to buy clothes, he would send me to pick the size off the racks inside the truck. I ran back and forth and up and down all day. I followed him for years.

One Saturday morning in August, I woke up to the sound of my father leaving with my then 19-year-old sister Felicia. He was going to check out a permanent store front for his booming clothing business. I waived them goodbye, not knowing that that would be the last time I ever would see my father alive. That day, a 15-year-old male shot and killed my father in front of my sister. Mom was now widowed with eight children, and my dreams of going to medical school looked bleak. I worked as a waitress the rest of my years in high school and graduated in the top 75 of my class. I did not have the funds to go to medical school, so I continued to work my way through nursing school and landed a great job at Jackson Memorial Hospital. Gun violence changed the trajectory of my life, but it never deterred me from seeking success.

For a time, all seemed right working twelve hour shifts per day, living in a comfy apartment in Miami Lakes, and being free and single, but I decided that I wanted to buy a house, so I started working in home health in addition to working at the hospital. Before I knew it, five years had passed, and I had a Bachelor of Science degree under my belt. I ventured off into home healthcare management. Over the next three years in home healthcare working as an administrator, I was able to complete a Master of Science degree in Nursing and an Advanced Registered Nurse Practitioner Degree. After achieving my goals of completing my graduate studies, my desire changed to financial self-sufficiency. My thoughts centered around being able to make enough money to secure a future for myself and my children without working the hours that I was required to work at that time. Through these thoughts, emerged a dream of owning a home health care agency. Working for several national homecare agencies, I had developed a knowledge of the financial operations. As a dedicated, loyal, and competent employee, I had made those agencies lots of money. I had worked in the nursing profession for ten years at that point and was quite content with my responsibilities and six-figure salary. The agency I worked for during the time was one of the largest nationally known home healthcare companies in the United States.

One day, after having my second child Alyssa, I started thinking about my future again and how I wanted to be free from working for someone else for the rest of my life. I was a nurse, stuck in administration and unable to spend quality time with my children. I had sinking feelings that I was missing out on my children's lives by being a working mother. My oldest daughter Amanda took her first steps in the presence of my mother who babysat her while I worked. I struggled with being a working mom and I wanted everything that stay-at-home moms had, but I could not achieve that because of my corporate lifestyle. Although I was great at my job, I felt that something was lacking in my soul. There was a feeling of restlessness each time the idea of venturing out on my own came to mind. Letting go of my job was akin to letting go of a security blanket. I was fearful of failing, but the more I thought about it, giving it a try was my only option. Against the odds and with lots of naysayers in my ears, I left my job and never looked back.

The vision started with a very basic business plan, jotting down ideas and conservatively estimating what I thought my capabilities would be in the first five years of business. An internet search led me to the Small Business Association (SBA) website. The site allowed me to identify all the banks who were lending to small businesses in the area. Off I went driving to West Palm Beach in pursuit of my first business loan. As a Director and Administrator, giving speeches and presenting to large groups was easy for me.

However, giving a presentation to two bankers who were very shrewd and un-emotional was totally different. As I finished, there were no applauds or accolades, just defining silence. I swallowed and waited to hear the word no! The Vice President sitting there said *"You are very confident, and we like the fact that you clearly have a good working knowledge of your business. The figures also look good. We know that you asked for $250,000 but we can start you off with $125,000 based on your credit score of 780. We will give you a signature loan at the maximum amount without needing assets to secure it."* Needless-to-say, I accepted! ...and began the creation of 'South Florida Pediatric Homecare'! As I was leaving the bank that day, so many thoughts crossed my mind. People said getting money to start a business would be difficult, but it seemed like the process went very smooth. Little did I know that feeling of ease would change in a short period of time... With a 780-credit score and a dream, my vision finally became a reality! I had my grand opening in June of 2001.

In the beginning, it was just my mom and I. Friends and family members would tell me that I was crazy to leave my comfy, good-paying, six-figured job. My mom would see the look of frustration on my face when people would say that, so she said to me, *"I know you. ...and if I had to bet on anyone, I'd bet on you, because I know that you will do anything that you set your mind to achieve."* With mom by my side, I tackled my first goal, which was to pursue contracts with major insurance carriers. This was my first business and I was aware that insurance contracts paid slowly: 60 to 90 days on most and some up to 120 days. After eight months in, with 30 employees and a constant flow of referrals, the money was tight. I used all my personal savings to make payroll until the checks from the insurance companies finally came in. My company would go from 0 dollars in revenue to $404,000 in revenue in my first year! However, that $125,000 SBA loan alone could not sustain my business, so I went back to the same bank that gave me the first loan, but since my company was less than a year old, they could not lend me more money until I had more time being established. This began my search for other lending sources to help support my company. I was turned down by bank after bank and I was so used to hearing "no" that I had become numb to it. I never realized that being a Black woman in business was such a disadvantage when it came to lending. I paid my bills on time, never wrote bad checks, and put everything I owned on the line to make my dream a reality. Yet that was not enough to prove to a bank that I was creditworthy.

The system of lending, forces new entrepreneurs to leverage their personal assets and put every debt of the business in their personal names. Therefore, the debt-to-income ratio increases, and a person's credit suffers due to over leveraging. It appeared simple to solve, but was unattainable for a young black female entrepreneur. I thought a "no" from a banker was the worst thing I could ever hear. Shockingly, I met with a Black banker who told me that I was a unicorn and that he had never seen a Black business achieve the level of success that mine had done in such a short period of time. Although he meant that as a compliment, I was offended because that meant that his expectations for Black businesses succeeding was low. While my company had a solid start and a strong vision for the future, I believed that there were many other Black success stories that existed besides mine.

The lending nightmares led me to pursue other sources. That is where a very small local business lender came in. Metro Broward was a program designed to give cashflow to small startups on a revolving basis to help with payroll or other expenses until their account receivables would come in. I presented my business plan with my actual revenue and Accounts Receivable to Metro Broward. There, I found a group of Board Members with experience and knowledge about small businesses that proved invaluable. They granted me a $35,000 line of credit, which I was able to use to get me through the

> *"The system of lending, forces new entrepreneurs to leverage their personal assets and put every debt of the business in their personal names."*

tight spots until the checks came in. I paid them back, but I did this for three more years.

My company's gross revenue at the end of 2004 was 3.1 million dollars. However, I still struggled to find lending institutions because the bigger the revenue, the more money you must spend. In 2005, just as I thought the business was doing great, Hurricane Wilma hit and dealt the business a huge blow. Our office flooded and the billing computers were wet from the windows breaking in our building. We were without power for nine days and without phones for 27 days. Meanwhile, business had to go on, so I returned to Metro Broward for help. At this point, my accounts receivables were backing up. Medicaid reform took place at the same time and caused the state to pay us extremely slow. Although I had 1.1 million dollars in accounts receivables, I knew that they were not coming in overnight. My payroll at that time was approximately $118,000 per week and my cash flow was tight. The small lending program said that I had outgrown their ability to lend based on the amount of working capital I needed, but they found a way to work with another local lending partner to help me buy my first building, move my company, and obtain an additional $270,000 in working capital. If it were not for this kind and concerned mentor's quick thinking and his ability to work with others in the community, I may have been one of those tragic business failures that we often hear and read about. Instead, I am in my 19th year of business and still standing strong!

Success does not come without its fair share of hard work and sacrifice. I learned long ago that discipline and consistency in my approach to life and business has propelled me to this point. There are three attributes on the next page that I have used in my life and in business to get ahead and stay that way. They are:

1. **Positive thoughts**

    Have you ever desired something but thought it may be too far out of reach for you to achieve? I believe that by thinking positively about your life and business, you get back what you project out. If you think you can achieve something and are willing to put in the work, you will achieve it. If you allow your thoughts to stagnate your will, your goals will never come to fruition.

2. **Patience**

You must be patient with yourself. Oftentimes, when we are venturing out as entrepreneurs, we can be very tough on ourselves. We want things to happen overnight. We have high expectations, but we must realize that everything takes time. If you are not patient, you will burnout and become stressed out. This may cause you to miss out on seeing the reward.

3. **Passion**

Do not take on a business endeavor that you are not passionate about or knowledgeable about. For example, I would never go into a restaurant business because I don't know a thing about running a restaurant. With passion, you are more invested in what you decide to pursue. Your passion will compel you to success.

While I believe that everyone and everything has value, they must be identified in a couple categories. Based on that, I have placed a tremendous amount of value on identifying the people in my life and understanding their placement based on value. The most valuable and important individuals are those who form your base of support. These are the people you can depend on in your time of need and in your time of rising. Whether it be on a professional, personal, or (in my case) a political level. They can be family or long-time proven friends. For example, my mother supported me even when some of my family and friends did not. There were so many people telling me that I had made a bad decision to leave my company to start my business, but it was my mother who said that if she had to bet on anyone, it would be on me! She further said, *"...so do what you need to do, and I will be right here!"*

As an entrepreneur, you must have a spirit of discernment when it comes to people who seek to attach themselves to you. I have made the mistake many times of using the term "friend" for people I became acquainted with in business. It's sad to say, but there are people who enter your life for what they can gain. Those people are not true friends. You must know the difference between the two. A friendship is a two-way street. Friends may be able to gain something from you, but you are able to gain something from them as well. Some people are genuinely interested in seeing you prosper, and they have no ulterior motive. They may be able to expand your network and put you in touch with the next group of people because they genuinely want to see you succeed. Use your discernment to see people for who they truly are.

I have learned that there will be times when those you think will be there for you when you really need them are nowhere to be found, but the ones you least expect, or don't even think about, will be there when you are in need. Therefore, the next set of people are those who are acquaintances. They stand in the role of uplifting you. You may only speak with these people infrequently, but you can rely on them to uplift you and cheer you on in the darkest times. These may be co-workers or other business owners who can relate to your tests and trials. They have a kinship by experience and therefore a greater understanding of whatever situation you are going through. Many times, these are members of a business networking group or chamber of commerce. When they see you in need, they may have resources or a network to introduce you to and thereby expand yours. I had two such people in my life like this. Both were from lending institutions and took an interest in helping me succeed.

Lastly, you must identify those who are not for you at all. Do this quickly and spare yourself the pain of disappointment and hurt. These are the people that may laugh and talk with you in your face, but when you leave, they talk negatively about you behind your back. These are judgmental people who will have you thinking that your life is terrible and theirs is perfect; meanwhile it's the opposite. Understand that they too have value and you must put them in the appropriate place in your life. This is not to say to not speak to them but be strategic with what you say to them. Otherwise, you may not like the way your words come back to you. The point I make is once you have identified these groups of people, continue to hone your identification skills and make it a lifelong practice. Sometimes as women or leaders in general, we miss the identifier's that dictate where we should place people in our lives. Appropriately assigning roles makes life easier and less complicated when it comes down to making decisions to discuss issues.

In 2005, my friends and neighbors convinced me to run for political office because I was always advocating for people or solving problems in my community. I desired to give back to my community as my father did, but I knew advocacy was my strong suit; so I chose the political path to give back, serve, and add value to the lives of others. I ran for office and lost twice. I won on my third try and have been serving as an elected official for 12 years now. I've had the pleasure of being nominated to serve as Broward County's (Florida) first African American female Mayor as well as the first African American female President of the Florida Association of Counties. I have a true nature for giving and healing. My Doctorate Degree in Nursing and my 28 years in healthcare, has provided me an opportunity to take my family morals and values and apply them to the lives of an entire county. By advocating for others, I give back and add value in my community.

At the end of the day, you must ask yourself "Am I happy?" You must be able to honestly answer this most basic question. When you can answer honestly, you can come to clarity on what you want out of life and what fulfills your soul. My soul fills from the joy of helping others. My father had a full-time business and ran a church food bank on the side. I spent a lot of time giving back, and so it was natural that I had the passion within me to help others.

As of this writing (July, 2021), and even with the damaging effects of COVID, South Florida Pediatric Homecare Inc. is recognized as one of the largest providers of Pediatric Homecare in Broward County. I am thankful every day for the insight, foresight, knowledge, and support I have received. I am now a President/CEO. One of my proudest achievements is the fact that through the success of my business, I was able to be present in the lives of my children. I was a classroom mom in all three of my children's classes for many years, and my business allowed me the freedom to achieve that. Vision can lead to having it all!

About the Author
Wendell Locke, Esq.

 Wendell was born and raised in West Palm Beach, Florida and matriculated in the Palm Beach County School System. He is a successful attorney, owner of an independent pharmacy and building contractor. He received his Doctorate of Pharmacy Degree from Florida A&M University's College of Pharmacy & Pharmaceutical Sciences in 1994, and his Juris Doctorate from the University of Miami School of Law in 1997. After graduating law school, Wendell worked for a few of the largest and most prestigious law firms in the United States and the world, representing various fortune 100 companies.

Wendell is admitted to practice in all Florida state courts, the United States' District Courts for the Southern, Middle and Northern Districts, the Court of Appeals for the Eleventh Circuit and before the United States Patent and Trademark Office.

He has represented clients throughout the state in various practice areas including, but not limited to, commercial litigation, corporate transactions, healthcare discipline defense, products liability, personal injury, automobile negligence, civil rights and, for those who might have encounters with law enforcement, criminal defense.

Wendell has also owned an independent pharmacy for the past eleven years (as of this writing) and continues to serve the community by helping those in need of his services.

Wendell is married with three beautiful children and currently resides in South Florida.

Chapter 2
Jumping Into Unchartered Waters
to Start a Business

Wendell Locke, Esq.
Pharmacist, Attorney & General Contractor

My siblings and I were told to go to school, get a college degree, and then get a good job. That was the path to success, so that was what I did. Entrepreneurship was not a common word used with people in my circles, and no one told me to pursue becoming a business owner. However, I knew at a young age about making money on my own without having a boss and punching a time clock for an employer. At the age of about ten or eleven, my mom would take me to the swap shop to sell things that I had fixed. I would find things, repair them, and sell them there. She supported me by sitting out there with me for hours. I did not make lots of money, but that was the beginning of making a little money using the skill of repairing things.

When I was in high school, my father told me that our house needed painting, that I was going to paint it, and that he would pay me. It took some time to paint the house alone, but other homeowners would drive by and ask that I stop by their homes to provide them a quote for painting their houses. I painted several of the neighbors' houses, and because there was so much work, I was able to pay some of my friends to help me. I was paid approximately $1,250-$1,400 per house and the homeowners were responsible for purchasing their own primer and paint. My friends would do the "cutting" around the windows and doors and I would roll the walls. I was able to easily pay my friends $250 apiece and would net no less than $700 per house. It was during that time that I learned that if I provided a service that people needed, I could make money.

CHOOSING THE RIGHT PATH

Entrepreneurship is the path to becoming wealthy. One can make a good living working on a job, but you can actually get wealthy through entrepreneurship. Not very many people can get wealthy working on a job. I have three careers, and I am active in all three. I am a trial and appellate lawyer; I am also a licensed pharmacist, and I am a building contractor. I graduated from FAMU with a Doctorate Degree of Pharmacy in 1994, then I graduated from the University of Miami School of Law in 1997 with a Juris Doctorate Degree. As of this writing (July, 2021), I have been a pharmacist for 27 years and I have been practicing law for 24 years now. Many ask why I went to law school after graduating with a degree in pharmacy, since I could make a comfortable living working in the pharmaceutical industry. There were a few reasons, including questioning whether I could work as a pharmacist for the rest of my life. Prior to entering pharmacy school, I thought that pharmacists would have a greater involvement in the decision-making process with patients, but that was not the case at the time. The profession of pharmacy was in transition to what I thought it would be. Pharmacists worked primarily in either retail drug stores or hospitals and had minimal contact with physicians. Things are different today and there much more pharmacy involvement. Hospitals have established medical teams where the pharmacists work hand in hand with the nursing staff and medical staff to provide services to patients, whereas when I was a pharmacy student, pharmacists were almost exclusively dispensing medication. It was in pharmacy school where I first heard of a "clinical pharmacist," but in hospital

> *"I learned that if I provided a service that people needed, I could make money."*

pharmacy practice, clinical pharmacists were not common. The other role of pharmacists that I knew about was retail pharmacy, which I did not want to do. At that time, I considered getting an MBA to compliment my pharmacy degree. I was not going to abandon my pharmacy degree, but since I was already drawn to business, the initial goal was to work on Wall Street as an investment banker with expertise in the pharmaceutical industry. I still would have used my pharmacy degree, but in an unconventional way. During my research, I stumbled across an interesting article that compared a law degree to an MBA. That was when I concluded that I could do everything with a law degree that a person could do with an MBA, and more.

Intellectual property law caught my attention. There were a small number of attorneys admitted to the patent bar. I also considered corporate transactions, sports and entertainment, and even real estate, but I gravitated to litigation. I saw it as a transferable skill that would enable me to also help people in my community. I did not know many Black people that needed legal services for mergers and acquisitions, public offerings or commercial real estate transactions. However, I did know people in my community who had a need for legal services for slip and falls, car accidents, contractors running off with their money, divorces, child custody disputes, etc. I believed that if I knew how to litigate, i.e., draft a complaint, respond to a complaint, prepare interrogatories, prepare requests for production, prepare requests for admissions, prepare responses to interrogatories, prepare responses to requests for production and prepare requests for admissions, take and defend a deposition, draft and respond to a motion, conduct legal research and go to trial (which required learning the rules of evidence). I could handle almost any civil, criminal, family and probate case. Litigation was the path I took, but I continued to practice pharmacy 3-4 times a month to keep my hands in the profession.

During my first two years of law school, I worked as a pharmacist during the day and attended law school in the evenings. I landed a summer internship at a big law firm in Miami after my second year of law school. At the end of the internship, the firm offered me a job after graduation. That prompted me to switch to law school full time and work as a staff relief pharmacist in the evenings and on weekends. I graduated during the summer of 1997, a few days before taking the Bar exam. While at the firm, I attended various law conferences with the goal of procuring my own clients. I felt that if I had my own clients, I could control my future professionally. Also, while at the firm, I observed that there were partners and then there were PARTNERS. For example, when certain PARTNERS walked into a room, people immediately straightened up and all eyes were on them. The other partners carried the same title, but the response was different. I quickly learned that there were three types of partners: The first type were those who could generate lots of work. I call those the *rainmakers* because they made money for the firm by bringing in clients with needs for legal services. The second type was a service partner. These partners did not have clients of their own, but they provided the legal services sought by the clients brought to the firm by the rainmakers. The third type of partner were those who had a unique set of skills that the clients needed but very few could provide. Attorneys with those particular skills were limited. They had expertise in a particular area. Because of that, when a partner had a client that needed that particular skill, those attorneys were the only options. That confirmed my initial thought that having the skillset is important, but to have the most control over your future, you must also invest time and energy in client development. Procuring my own clients would put me in control of my future.

I have worked for some of the largest firms in the country and each firm provided its own unique experience. I learned a lot, including my own style of practicing law. I noticed that most of the in-house lawyers who were in positions to retain outside counsel did not look like me. I had some success in getting my own clients, but I found it oftentimes difficult to establish substantive relationships with many in-house attorneys because our backgrounds were significantly different.

After working at different law firms, observing things and gaining experience, the thought of me starting my own firm was constantly in the back of my mind. One of the things that stood out to me the most while working at the large law firms was the fact that the clients we were serving were primarily corporations and wealthy individuals. We were not serving people from my community. There were some instances where I had opportunities to help people, but my firm did not allow me to take on those representations because they did not fit within the criteria of the firm. I finally made the decision to branch out on my own when a family member was in need of legal help and my employer would not allow me to help him. I had to make a decision between staying with the firm or helping my family member when he needed me the most. I decided to leave the big firm and have never looked back.

SHUTTER HANGERS

The first business that I actually registered with the state was Shutter Hangers, Inc., which still exists. This business was birthed out of a need that many people would have in South Florida during hurricane season. I saw a need that I knew I could potentially fulfill. Anyone familiar with hurricane shutters, knows that after Hurricane Andrew ravished South Florida in 1992, building departments in South Florida counties required new homes to include hurricane shutters. Most new home builders included panel hurricane shutters, which were made with either aluminum or steel and were the least expensive option. While panel hurricane shutters are very effective in protecting the windows and doors from the debris and high-speed winds, attaching them to the openings of doors and windows is difficult and risky, as the panel shutters are heavy, the edges of them are very sharp, and attaching them oftentimes requires the use of a latter and more than one person. While at the home of an acquaintance, I overheard someone complain about how difficult it was to attach the panel hurricane shutters to the openings of their windows and doors, that they did not have all the necessary tools, it took the entire day, and that the male spouse had sustained a sizeable cut on his hands and arms in the process. After hearing a few of the other couples discuss how difficult it was for them also to attach the panel hurricane shutters to the openings of their windows and doors, or how the thought of work associated with it overwhelmed them, I asked the question, *"How much would you be willing to pay someone to attach the panel hurricane shutters to the openings of the windows and doors, and then take them down for you after the storm was over?"* The responses were surprising, as many of them with large homes quickly agreed to pay up to $1,500, and those with the smaller homes agreed to pay about $1,000. What caught my attention was that I knew that I could round up a crew of four to five men who could attach the panel hurricane shutters to the openings of their windows and doors and then take them down after the storm has passed for no more than $500. That was the birth of Shutter Hangers.

After establishing Shutter Hangers, I was trying to get work through the local school district for my law practice. When I looked for RFPs on the website for legal services, I happened to see that they were looking for someone to "activate" hurricane shutters. The school district had a contract where certain schools would be used as storm shelters for hurricanes. When they called, they needed all shutters in the schools closed within eight hours. Shutter Hangers was the only company to submit a bid on the contract. The contract had two parts: maintenance and activation. Had I gotten the whole bid, I would have made about $120,000 annually without ever facing an actual hurricane, and more if called to active the shutters, but the school district did not want only one provider to have that contract, so they opened up the bid, but I ended up getting a big chunk of the contract. I was an attorney, but I saw an opportunity and I acted on it. Shutter Hangers is still active, but it is incorporated into my general construction now.

When I first branched out to start my own law practice, I wanted to get a few Black male attorneys together to start a law firm because I knew other skilled lawyers. In my mind, we would go after both commercial work and corporations while also serving our people. I had envisioned about five lawyers. Of the individuals that I had in mind, one had real-estate experience, one would do the corporate transactional work, and the rest of us would litigate, take cases to trial and handle appeals. Unfortunately, many of us are not used to coming together and working together. Everyone seemed to love the idea, but it was a challenge getting everyone to sit down together and discuss it. There were people who had the skillsets to do it, but it never happened.

STARTING MY OWN FIRM

The first thing I did when starting my law firm was secure office space. Then, I registered with the state and secured my employer identification number from the IRS. I initially secured a post office box, opened a business account, then got business cards printed. Getting business cards was significant because I needed to pass them out to people that I would meet. I have discovered that meeting and giving people your card does pay off. Some people might not call you right away, but at some point down the line, they will call you or they will refer you to someone who needs your services. I was just starting out and wanted to be flexible and fluid. Once I went on my own, I made it a point to be visible. I would go places and meet people. I would speak to them about what I did and would give them my card. I aggressively networked and tried to figure out a way to get plugged into various business circles. From time to time, I would get commercial work, but the bulk of my work came from Black people in need of legal services. A lot of the larger clients did not use me after I went out on my own because they could not justify using a solo practitioner to handle their employers' legal matters on certain issues.

My legal work comes from different places. In the beginning, I had mostly civil cases but would also take on family and criminal cases. I realized that there were a lot of people who needed lawyers but could not afford them. I wanted to help my people, so when clients did not have the money that a traditional law firm would charge, I would work with them on payment plans or they would pay a portion up front and then pay a certain amount each month. Most of my business stemmed from word-of-mouth referrals, and still does. I still get calls from a billboard that I had put up in Miami several years ago.

HIGHLIGHTS OF PRACTICING LAW

Some of my most gratifying moments as an attorney have been times when I have helped to address gaps in the law. There are some issues within the law that typically are not to the advantage of Black people, and if lawyers lack the courage to address them, those issues go unaddressed. I am proud of the fact that I have had the courage to raise some of those issues. Of course, those are not popular stances, but I have gotten people out of situations where, but for my assistance, they likely would have gone to prison. I have gotten recoveries for clients whose rights were violated, and I have helped some fathers reunite with their children who were being denied access to them. Days like those make practicing law worthwhile for me.

THE RETAIL PHARMACY

About 11 years ago, I was approached by a former colleague about the idea of opening an independent pharmacy. We had previously worked together as pharmacists at an overnight pharmacy. His argument was that pharmacies were doing very well and he felt that we could go into business together and make money. After considering it, I thought that it would be a good business move, so we found a space at a reasonable price on a major street. The location we found had previously been approved as a pharmacy, so we lucked out in finding that spot. However, many municipalities had moratoriums that were preventing pharmacies from opening at the time because of all the pill mills that were popping up left and right. We managed to navigate through that and were still able to open. After we were approved by the city to open, we completed an application with the state and then bought the software that allowed us to bill insurance companies. We acquired our inventory, hired a pharmacist and opened up. Prior to hiring a full-time pharmacist, my colleague and I split time covering the store. We also split responsibilities. Pharmacy is a heavily regulated profession, so I deal with administrative and regulatory things such as the Board of Pharmacy, the DEA, audits from insurance companies, licensing and reconciling of the finances. My partner deals with the day-to-day logistics. He may flag down an audit or remind us that it is time to update our insurance, certificates, etc. He reads and responds to emails and works from his computer.

As of this writing, we are contemplating selling or closing the business because the margins are getting so tight; and the audits are more and more intense to the degree to where we are barely making money. I am now constantly asking myself if it is still worth it. We are at the 11th year mark now, but the regulations that are put in place seem to favor big pharmacies with a focus of pushing smaller independent pharmacies, like us, out. I could have a patient who loves coming to my pharmacy, but her insurance company requires her to use its own mail order pharmacy service, unless she is willing to pay out of pocket and get reimbursed from her insurance company three months later. It is awful because even though a person may love my services, they cannot use me because they cannot afford to pay out of pocket then wait to get reimbursed at a later date. It is not a good climate for independent pharmacies right now. My partner is in agreement. He sees what is going on in the industry as well.

ADVICE TO ASPIRING ENTREPRENEURS

There is a litany of ways you can make money. My advice is to do your research in the area in which you intend to go. With the internet, that is not a difficult task, but some people have analysis paralysis. We think too long and will sit on an idea for years because we feel like we don't have enough information. If you have an idea, act on it and do something towards keeping it at the forefront your mind every day. Don't procrastinate. To the extent that you must align yourself with people, make sure they are people who have your best interest at heart, so that you can achieve success. Don't think that everyone will be happy to see you succeed. Everyone will not be happy for you and everyone will not always support you, but that is okay. Just keep moving forward. Success is the best response!

About the Author
Lakitsia Gaines

 Lakitsia Gaines is an Insurance and Financial Services Agent in the South Florida region. She is a native of Miami, FL and graduated from Florida A&M University in Tallahassee. Lakitsia currently owns offices in South Miami and Hallandale Beach, Florida and she is one of the top 20 trainee agents in the country. For eleven years, she has been in the Chairman's Circle and has received the National Multiline Sales Award, the National Sales Achievement Award and has been a Silver Scroll Qualifier since 2016. Lakitsia is also a member of the internationally coveted Million Dollar Roundtable (MDRT), which represents the top ½ percent of insurance and financial services professionals in the world. In 2016, Mrs. Gaines qualified for the Presidents Club in Life Insurance, which represents the top 50 agents across the country and given by the CEO of her organization.

Lakitsia has been recognized as 'Business Firm of the Year', 'Most Influential and Prominent Black Women in Business and Leadership' and the coveted 'In the Company of Women Awards' as an Outstanding Woman of Business and Economics. She has spoken at the International Black Enterprise Women of Power Summit, been featured on the Steve Harvey Morning Show, and twice on the Power Stage at the Essence Festival in Louisiana. Lakitsia is a member of Miami Biscayne Bay (FL) Chapter of The Links, Inc., The Miami Alumnae Chapter of Delta Sigma Theta Sorority, Inc. and Antioch Missionary Baptist Church. She also serves as a board member for many nonprofits. She personally donates more than $50,000 a year in sponsorships and scholarships for deserving high school students. Her personal motto is, "People don't care how much you know, until they know how much you care." She and her husband Shawn have two children: Kendall and Kaitlyn.

Chapter 3

The Art of Maintaining a
Successful Business

Lakitsia Gaines

Insurance and Financial Services Agent

W hen you step onto the path that has been preordained for you, you will flourish because that is "your" path. Stepping out in faith to start my own business has been deeply rewarding, but make no mistake, there have been some pitfalls and obstacles. As an insurance and financial services agent for one of the largest insurance companies in the country and having been in the business for over 20 years, I have learned a thing or two, and I have no problem sharing some of the things that I have learned. Running a business is not for the weak or those who give up easy. It is for the strong-willed, the committed, those who know how to grind, and those who know how to overcome challenges and learn from them.   Currently, I have two Florida Insurance and Financial Services offices in different counties: Miami Dade and Broward. I have 15 employees who speak Russian, French, Spanish, Creole, English. However, they all know how to speak MONEY! Yes, they speak money. We provide over 200 products including mortgages, home owner's insurance, mutual funds, bonds, auto insurance, life insurance, college plans, retirement plans, etc.

HOW IT ALL BEGAN

After graduating summa cum laude from Florida Agricultural and Mechanical University (FAMU) with a degree in journalism and a minor in Spanish, I had ten job offers, and most were from reputable companies. While trying to decide which one to take, my wise mother gave me some good advice. She told me to go with the larger company, because at the time, the CEO offered the employees a 401k retirement plan and also gave gifts and birthday cards to the employees. Since mama knows best, I took the position with this company because it was the largest, the oldest and the most established in the industry. I started off as a claims representative in Miami. From the time I took that position, my career took off. I received promotion after promotion. After about nine months, I was promoted to a Claims Specialist and relocated to Winter Haven, Florida, only to be promoted again a few months later to a Public Affairs position. In that position, I was the voice of the company. After that, I was promoted to work at the first satellite office in Miami, then off to our corporate office in Bloomington, IL, and finally Woodbury, MN, with a team of people who reported to me. At the time, I managed communications for six states and was responsible for all of the media relations for the company. I also oversaw community sponsorships and alliances.

SEEDS PLANTED

I was once again offered another promotion as a Communication Strategist for the Chairman's Council in Illinois. While transitioning into this position, I met my husband Shawn. He was working in Human Resources for the same company when he called me to set up house hunting in Illinois. We began dating, got married in Miami, and then we moved to Minnesota. We have now been married for 20 years (as of this writing). Kendall, our son was born a year and a half after we moved, and Kaitlyn, our daughter was born two years after that. While in Minnesota, I met an African American company executive who had an impression on me. As an insurance agent and a financial planner, she had been very successful in the company and had made the company lots of money. She told me that she thought I would be a successful agent and that I should consider becoming one. She saw something in me that I did not see in myself at the time. She asked me to consider pursuing it. Interestingly, she had not been the first to plant that seed in me. However, at the time, I was afraid of taking that leap. I did not have the confidence to be my own agent, but I did think long and hard about it. I thought about the fact that I had been working 70 hours each week and I really wanted the freedom to manage my own time. I was connected to a phone because if the media called, I had to be there instantly. I wanted control of my own calendar. I also wanted family balance because I was married with a new baby and I needed to spend more time with my family. I was not able to spend as much time with my son and my husband as I wanted to. Additionally, working for the company in the capacities that I had worked, I knew what community causes were important to them, and I wanted to be able to give back to the community causes that were important to me. ...so, after thinking long and hard about becoming an agent and considering all those elements, I decided to pursue it.

BECOMING AN AGENT

The company creates a pool of candidates who have been vetted to become agents, and I did all that I needed to do to get in the pool to become approved. As a candidate, when the geographical location you want is ready, you then put your name in, and the executives will interview you. I interviewed five times before I was finally selected. While interviewing, one must convince the top executives that they have the skillset, the adeptness, the competence, the ability to train a team, and the capability to be able to sell. The company is particular about their brand, so they review each person carefully, scrutinizing their track records, finances, competencies, sales experiences, skillsets, etc. It was during my fifth interview that I came with undeniable passion. I wanted to be an agent in South Florida, and it finally became available for me to open in March, 2006. However, when I was selected, there were also five others to split the business. This meant that the South Miami opening had to be divided up among the six of us. We each had a geographical area of concentration. Each of us were required to hire our own people, develop our own training manuals, invest our own monies into the business and secure our own locations. We were also responsible for all revenue and expenses.

DEVELOPING THE BUSINESS FOUNDATION

In preparing to become an agent, the first thing I did was see an accountant to discuss the tax entities available to business. At the time, there were a few types: S Corp, C Corp, LLC, and a Sole Proprietor. I filed as an S Corp because of the tax benefits and liability. I did this because if there is ever an issue with the business, the liability stays within the business and does not carry over into my personal or family assets. Because of an S Corp, many business owners have been able to file bankruptcy many times since filing bankruptcy does not affect your personal assets. It affects the business only because it is a standalone entity. Filing with the IRS allowed me to establish credit, open a bank account and establish assets. I applied for and received an American Express card, did some renovations, switched over the lights and telephone lines, bought some office furniture, and did everything else necessary to get started. I then began looking for employees. I advertised in newspapers, on websites, with churches, through referrals, and used Indeed and Career Builder websites. It was in August of 2005 when I got approved to become an agent, so I gave myself a timeline for when I wanted to open my doors. I also had smaller timelines identified for other decisions that needed to be made. I had a February, 2006 target date to have all of my decisions made, with March being my official opening

> *"I filed as an S Corp because of the tax benefits and liability. I did this because if there is ever an issue with the business, the liability stays within the business and does not carry over into my personal or family assets."*

month. Everyone had been hired and ready to start by the target date. During this time, Shawn and I had just relocated from Winter Haven, FL to South Florida and by this time, we had two children. My son and daughter are two years apart.

While working diligently on opening my new office, I also had things happening on the personal side. My husband and I were trying to get our new house situated and also working on getting the children into preschool. At the time, we had a three-year-old and a one year-old. We needed to get used to a new environment, find a church home, familiarize ourselves with the local grocery stores, shopping areas and everything necessary for getting acclimated to a new area. During this time, my husband Shawn was doing almost everything concerning the children. It was Shawn who potty trained our daughter. He was the one to take the children to school, and while I was working, he was home with them when he got off work. He referred to himself as President of single-married fathers' club because he assumed all of the responsibilities of the house and the children because I had an hour commute to and from work everyday and was putting in substantial hours each week. Shawn did a fantastic job with the children and all of the household responsibilities.

THE EXPECTATION OF MY DOWNFALL

In my first year, I grinded hard. Everyone was invisible to me. I had to prove myself to others, to the company, and most importantly, to myself. The criticisms and expectations of my downfall gave me the impetus to go hard for my business. I was determined to succeed. I would buy leads, read books on how to market and how to grow a business; I would teach myself strategies and techniques on how to be profitable in business and I would attend conferences. I would ask certain people specific things and I taught myself the art of reflection. I opened my doors in March 2006, worked extremely hard, and was number five in the country my first year!

Notwithstanding the significant success in my first year of business, there were those who were waiting for my downfall. I was not only disappointed, but a little hurt when an African American friend called me. Initially, I thought she was calling to welcome me to the area and to say that if there was anything I needed, she was there; but on the contrary, she was calling because she wanted me to know that she (and others) had a relationship with one of the other five agents (another African American woman), and that their loyalty lied with that woman. She told me that, *"We will not treat you the same way we treat her, because we have a strong relationship with her."* That phone call discouraged me because I did not expect that from a sister, but I continued to grind. There was also a Hispanic male with an office about 20 minutes from me. He was successful in stealing my large clients. Some of my customers would tell me some of the things that he had told them about me. He would tell my customers that they needed to move their business to him because I was new, had no sales experience, was not strong enough to survive in the Miami environment, did not speak Spanish, did not know what I was doing, was going to fail, and would be gone in a year. He explained to them that they needed someone stable - like him. Some of my customers would just cancel their accounts with me and transfer them to him without even speaking with me. What was so frustrating is that he did not target my small customers. He went after my large clients.

I also learned that there were people only working for the money, but not willing to truly put in the work. Some did not want to report to me because I was half their age and some did not want to contribute to my success because I was not their race. I was also being criticized by the other agents that I shared the business with. Two of them were Cubans and since the Miami-Dade County area is proliferated with Cubans, they were very confident that I would not get business and would not be successful in the Miami area. They had shared their thoughts with a few other people, and it came back to me, but their criticism gave me the motivation to prove them all wrong. It propelled me to put my heart, mind, and soul into the success of my business. The naysayers made me stronger, wiser, and bolder.

GENUINE FRIENDS IN THE INDUSTRY

After finishing number five in the country in my first year, I have since, been one of the top-selling agencies in the world. Coming into the knowledge of those who were expecting my downfall, sent me into the prayer closet. I asked God to send genuine friends to me, those who truly cared about me and who would support me. He sent me a white female and a Hispanic male. The three of us are the best of friends to this day. We support each other, look after each other, share information and knowledge with each other, and are genuine friends. Our families have merged, and we have a bond like no other. We even made a pack with each other that if ever one of us were in a position where we could not manage our business temporarily, one of us would step in and manage the business for the other. That pack speaks volumes, because to trust someone to that magnitude with your business, speaks to the level of trust that the three of us have in each other. Never in a million years did I think that God would send me a White woman and a Hispanic man as the genuine friends that I prayed for, but when you ask God for something, don't be surprised at the package that He sends it to you in. Not only are we friends, but in business, the three of us were the top producers. Jim, Ellie and I were in The President's Club, which means that out of 20,000 agents, we were one of the top 50 across the country for production and sales results.

In year three, I was traveling across the country teaching other agents how to maximize their business. My profit margin was 92%. Once, while I was traveling to speak at a conference, I received notice that one of my employees had gone to work at the business down the street for the man who had stolen my large clients in my first year. He knew that I was out of town, so while I was gone, he came to my office to steal my employees, with an offer of two dollars an hour more. When I called the office to ask my staffer what had happened to my other employee and why was he leaving to go and work for the competitor, she said, *"Oh. about that…I wanted to tell you that I am leaving too."* After asking a few questions, I ascertained that it was because he had offered her two dollars an hour more as well. I told her that we could have a conversation about it when I returned, so that I could help her to have a smooth transition and to support her. I made sure that I was very caring and supportive while on the phone with her because I was out of town, and had I shown any emotion other than support and understanding, she could have easily sabotaged my business. However, upon my return, I terminated her on the spot. I did not want her to sabotage my office while I was out of town, so I placated her until I returned.

LEADERSHIP REFLECTION

Through reflection, I would ask myself the following questions:

1. What did I do well?
2. What do I need to eliminate (money, staff, systems, etc.)?
3. What do I want to keep, change, or add?

I once walked out of my office as my team was laughing amongst each other. When I asked them what they were laughing about, I was told this: *"When your ponytail is to the left, you are in a good mood and we know that we can talk to you and usually get what we want. When your ponytail is to the right, you are in a bad mood, and we know to stay away from you; and when it is in the middle, you are neutral, so we just play it safe."* My team had narrowed my leadership style down to emotional moodiness. Although I laughed with them, I viewed this revelation as a failure in leadership, because if I am not approachable or accessible as a leader, then how can I expect people to stay with me? I reflected real hard on that situation and had to face the harsh reality that I did have a high turnover rate. Over the course of my sixteen years in business now (as of this writing), I have hired about 80 people. When I would let some people go, I would say that I was glad that I got rid of that toxicity. However, going through people hurt the continuity of my business. I needed retention of my team members so that collectively, we are able to provide better service to our customers. That introspection helped me to become a better leader.

FAMILY IS THE PRIORITY, NOT MONEY

One of my biggest growing pains was the fact that I had to realize that in life, you do not get a second chance to make up lost time with your spouse and children. I was working so hard at being successful in business, thinking the whole time that I was doing this for my family, that they were resenting me as a wife and mother for being gone all the time. They didn't care about all the money I was bringing home. All they wanted was my time. What was important to them was family outings, dinner together, being on my husband's arm at events, talking about what was going on in their lives, etc. There were times that Shawn and I would go on trips, and he would be so happy that we were spending time together on those vacations, but while there, I would sleep the entire trip. I was not cooking, not spending time, was exhausted all the time, had no energy when I got home, and all this was taxing on the marriage. I had to get out of my own way and prioritize what was really important. I was a success in business, but in my mind, a failure in my personal life. I am thankful because I realize that family is the priority. Our relationships are so much stronger now.

ADVICE TO ASPIRING ENTREPRENEURS

When it is in your heart to do something, don't listen to the naysayers and don't get discouraged by those who may not help you. Set your goals, make your plan, and put yourself in position to succeed. It will take sacrifice and hard work, but if you are willing to put in the work and sacrifice all that needs to be done in order to succeed, you will eventually reap the rewards of your hard work. Don't give up because TRUST ME, you will exceed your wildest dreams!

About the Author
Brenda L. Hill-Riggins

Brenda L. Hill-Riggins is the CEO of MARS Contractors, Inc. She is a visionary businesswoman with domestic and international business interests. Since 1992, her company has partnered in construction projects costing over four billion dollars. Ms. Hill-Riggins is a philanthropic and innovative business owner who has diversified her businesses to include farming, life skills, coaching, and authorship. Her mission is to assist others with economic empowerment, job training, professional development, real estate development, and family community development.

Brenda has received honors from two United States' Presidents: President Obama's Lifetime Achievement Award and President Clinton's Letter of Recognition. She was also recognized by two City of Miami Mayors. Mayor Carlos Alvarez designated Brenda L. Hill-Riggins Day and Alexander Penelas recognized MARS Contractors for becoming the 23rd Fastest-Growing Inner City Business in America out of 2,000 according to Inc. Magazine and Harvard University. Brenda received an Honorary Degree in Philosophy from CICA International University and Seminary.

Brenda has published/written over 10 books, including co-authoring with Ken Blanchard and Stephen Covey. She has been featured in over 20 news articles; received more than 60 awards; patented or copyrighted more than 10 inventions; and created innovative educational programs. Brenda launched the MARS Trade Academy, offering apprenticeship programs in plumbing, HVAC, carpentry, electrical, and farming. Brenda is an international panelist who speaks and presents workshops and seminars to aspiring professionals and entrepreneurs. Running a construction company is what she does, but who she is? "The Vision Surrogate™."

Chapter 4
Birthing the Business Within You!

Brenda L. Hill-Riggins

President/CEO, MARS Contractors Inc.

B irthing a business is similar to birthing a baby. Prior to the baby being born, appropriate preparations must be made for the baby's arrival. Once the baby arrives, it must be fed, nurtured, carefully watched, and changed frequently. There is no difference with a business. It must be fed with constant and updated information, nurtured with innovative strategies, carefully watched to avoid costly mistakes, and changes must be periodically made.

Everyone is not meant to own a business. Out of every 100 people who start a business, only 5% of them will succeed. This is because not everyone has the acumen to ensure that their business can be a success. Entrepreneurship has to be in your DNA. As a die-hard business owner, dismantling your business should never come to mind when you face obstacles, setbacks or failures. Many people use the words "business owner" and "entrepreneur" interchangeably, but there is a marked difference between the two words. The difference between a business owner and an entrepreneur is this: One can be taught how to own a business, but one cannot be taught how to make strategic choices and decisions that will ensure success. Entrepreneurs have great insight, hindsight, and foresight.

I met my husband Marcus at a grocery store. He was finishing a five-year plumbing apprenticeship program in which he traveled 45 minutes to and from, two nights a week for five years. He was in the union making $15.16 per hour. We were married in a castle in April, 1993. The seed for starting our own business was planted when my husband shared with me his dream of having his own plumbing company one day. I accepted the charge to help him make his dream a reality and fulfill the promise that God made to him. I too had a goal of owning my own business, but my husband and I had two different reasons for why we wanted businesses. Marcus' goal was to own a plumbing company. My goal was to build a dynasty. A dynasty consists of several businesses. I operate from a dynastic perspective. I started the incorporation process for MARS Contractors Inc. in January of 1992. Our business is in Miami, Florida. We started as a plumbing company almost 30 years ago, in 1992. A few years later, Marcus secured his General Contractors, HVAC and underground utilities licenses. Presently we employ 20 employees with an anticipation of over 75 by the end of the 2021 year.

In preparing for our business, we sat down and developed a business plan. I merged my vision into the plan to begin building our dynasty. Together, we made a life plan that included both the business plan and a dynastic wealth plan. I had the vision of how it could be executed. I have the ability to decode dreams and turn them realities. The reason I wanted to start my own business was so I could better control my destiny and create a better life for my children and grandchildren.

STEPPING OUT ON FAITH

The first thing I did in stepping out on faith to pursue the business endeavor was talk to God about it. I asked for clarity and wisdom. I then weighed my options, sat down with a pen and paper, and began writing the goals, the action plans for each goal, and the timelines needed to accomplish each goal. I also conducted a personal evaluation of our strengths and weaknesses. My focus at the time was on creating balance between the mind, body, and spirit, and then follow what God said about order and priority.

RECOGNIZE YOUR SEASON

You must learn to recognize seasons of change. Doing this will teach you when to move and when not to move. Pay attention to trends in industries and in business. Hurricane Andrew, the most powerful tropical system to ever hit the state of Florida at the time, slammed down on Miami on August 24th of 1992, devastating the South area of Miami. It tore directly through South Miami Dade County - especially the small cities of Homestead and Florida City, stripping most homes of their roofs, including their concrete foundations. This hurricane took the lives of many, destroyed thousands of homes and businesses, uprooted trees, and left the three cities that received the brunt of the storm, in ruin. Prior to the hurricane, I had just lost my job at a law firm and was looking for employment. I had been working at that law firm as a file clerk on a new case the firm had just taken on. I started at $7.50 per hour with the promise that I would be making $12.00 an hour at the end of four months. My husband was a union member, working for a mechanical company, and they would send him out on various jobs. When one job ended, they would send him out on another job. During this time, he had been preparing to take the state of Florida Plumber's Construction Exam set for June, 1992. He had studied from January to June of that same year. His license came three days before the storm. This was our season!

According to the National Hurricane Center (NHC), when Hurricane Andrew hit, about 1.4 million people lost power; 25,524 homes were destroyed; and 101,241 others damaged. About 250,000 people were left homeless in Miami-Dade County. Immediate help was needed. We knew that we needed to do all we could to help our friends and neighbors, but we also knew that it was time to move forward with our business. After we did what needed to be done to officially set up and legitimize our business, we went to the Federal Emergency Management Agency (FEMA) meetings that were held in the aftermath of the storm. We wore black T-shirts, black pants, and steal-toe boots. While at those meetings, we introduced ourselves as MARS Plumbing to city officials and our new peers. Attending those meetings paid off. We received our first contract - in the midst of the aftermath of that devastating hurricane. Our very first contract was setting up temporary government office trailers for the cities of Florida City and Homestead. The office trailers needed to be connected to water and sewer, so we were contracted to do the connections. There were two separate trailers in two separate locations, so we worked on both. We borrowed the seed money of $5,000 from my husband's sister to get started. We completed the work within a couple weeks and paid her back within a month.

While working in that contract, we continued looking for others. We would attend the meetings that the commissioners were having in the various districts and handed out our flyers while introducing ourselves and our business. One day, while at the Miami-Dade Development offices, we learned about becoming certified as a minority-owned firm. A pathway was created for Blacks to participate on government projects. After registering, we were put in the database to be considered for future jobs. Ninety-nine percent of our work has been because of this certification process and catapulted us into becoming legitimate players in the game. Word of mouth was our best advertisement. We also received business when word got out among the construction industry. Since my husband had been part of the union, many of his former co-workers were recommending our company to others and were also sending business our way.

OBSTACLES AND HURDLES

Starting a business was not easy. We did run into obstacles and hurdles along the way, but we faced them, overcame them, and proceeded forward despite them. We learned that many in the industry have preconceived notions about Black-owned companies, making it a challenge to get bonded, financed, good labor, fair insurance rates, etc. We were bondable but getting bonded proved to be a major challenge. Not approving Black minority businesses to get substantial bonding, financing, insurance and the like, is a systematic process put in place to keep minority businesses into a certain financial box. We learned that Black businesses do not get the bonding that White companies get, and even today, it is still difficult for small minority businesses to get bonded.

Another source of frustration for our business were the audits. Audits that businesses face can be a major headache. They come from various avenues: IRS, insurance, labor department, union, and county. Audits are necessary and can be beneficial if you know how to benefit from them. They can help you to understand whether you are managing your business based on industry standards or not, but there are times when their findings are not accurate and a substantial amount of money is spent proving the errors of others. As business owners, we have gone through several audits with the IRS. The typical audit is for three years. In some circumstances such as foreign income or substantial underreporting, the IRS can audit you for six years.

When the matter involves an unfiled tax return or civil tax fraud, the IRS can audit you indefinitely. In other words, under the latter two scenarios, the statute of limitations would not expire. In 2016, the IRS went back to 1999 as a result of an audit and we were told that we owed over $171,000! We were threatened that they would lock the doors and shut us out of our own business if we didn't pay it. When this happens in typical business, the obvious and most reasonable thing to do, is for a business to pay a tax attorney lots of money to prove or disprove that the money is owed. However, we did not do that. I knew how attorneys worked. The cost would have been just as much as they alleged we owed, so after getting that report, I bought two books entitled, 'What the IRS Doesn't Want You to Know' and 'How to fight the IRS'. I read, studied, and educated myself, because I could not afford to hire someone to do it at the time. I went through every item that they noted. I dug deep and found what I needed to know about the noted areas. As a business owner for almost 30 years, my advice to every aspiring business owner or entrepreneur is to keep organized and accurate documentation. It is imperative that record-keeping is precise and kept in order. You will never know when you must prove your past actions and decisions. As a business owner, you must have the mindset of an attorney. After reading, studying, learning, and researching, I not only was able to prove that MARS Contractors did NOT owe the IRS $171,00, but I found out that they actually owed us over $40,000! As a business owner, you cannot afford NOT to do the following things:

1. Keep accurate records of everything!
2. Know the tax laws.
3. Know your rights.
4. Know that it takes courage to fight!
5. Most attorneys would fail an audit conducted on their own business, so study to show yourself approved.

Another obstacle that we faced was an audit from the labor department. There was a time when they physically went out to one of our sites and started interviewing our employees as they were working. They asked the employees all sorts of questions: *What is it that you actually do? How much do you get paid? Are you paid in cash?* etc. Afterwards, they came to us and accused the business of not paying our employees enough. They said, *"You are under-paying your employees by this amount, and you should be paying them at least this amount."* They then returned with a report indicating that we underpaid our employees over $130,000 and we had 30 days to pay the underpayments and fines. When businesses pay fines to the Labor Department, their penalty is about 30% in addition to the underpayment that they claim you owe. After receiving this report, I audited the auditor's audit and discovered that the amount that was

> *"...my advice to every aspiring business owner or entrepreneur is to keep organized and accurate documentation. It is imperative that record-keeping is precise and kept in order."*

underpaid was only $1,300, which was due to a mathematical error made by my office employee on the initial report.

That situation was a state audit, but there are also local audits. MARS Construction has had many different types of audits since we have been in business, and I have been able to prove them wrong each time because I have had the documentation to substantiate my position. Documentation and accurate record-keeping is crucial when in business! When it comes to the Labor Department, you must be able to prove by cancelled checks that you have paid your employees the true amount due them. One of the reasons why many construction companies find themselves in trouble is because some pay workers in cash; so when they get audited, they do not have the paperwork to prove that they have complied with the Department of Labor. Unfortunately, they end up paying substantial fines. Operate your business the right way and learn how to protect your assets!

OUTSOURCING

Outsourcing is a familiar concept to many entrepreneurs. Small companies routinely outsource their payroll processing, accounting, distribution, and many other important functions for various reasons. It is important to keep in mind that whether you sign a contract to have another company perform the functions of an entire department or single task, you are turning the management and control of a function that comes out of your company over to another company. The outsourcing company will be driven to make a profit from the services that they are providing to you and other businesses like yours, and they are motivated by profit. There are times that they need to be audited too and their work needs to be checked. Make sure you understand the contract and do not be afraid to negotiate the terms.

Although you have hopefully outlined expectations in your contract, unless you monitor for compliance with those expectations, you will have no way of knowing whether those expectations are being met. If those expectations are not being met, the availability, efficiency, and effectiveness of your operations as well as the security of your systems and data can be impacted. Outsourcing can be very convenient and allows you to focus on the day-to-day innerworkings of the business, but when you outsource, you are not learning. The company you are outsourcing to is doing all the work and more often than not, without any oversight. For example, for payroll, many people use ADP and Paychex. Because businesses rely on these outsourcing companies to take out the appropriate amount of taxes, FICA, etc. They totally rely on these companies. I routinely audit the payroll company that I outsource to.

As a business owner, there are certain things that you will learn along the way. Sometimes you learn the hard way, but if you are proactive, you alleviate many of those headaches. For example, the day you hire your first employee, you immediately become responsible for payroll tax. Despite the name, payroll tax is not a single tax, but a blanket term used to refer to all taxes paid on the wages of employees. When you have employees, you are responsible for deducting a portion of employee wages to pay certain taxes on their behalf and paying payroll taxes on each of your employees out of the business revenue. You must know the tax rates. There is a current tax rate for social security for the employee, one for Medicare for the employee, you the employer, and the combined, etc. The tax laws change, so as an employer, it is critical to know what the changes are. Don't always rely on those you outsource to. Review their work from time to time. Another important, yet valuable tidbit for you to know, is the formula for how payroll companies engage you. When you know the formula for how they audit you, you can turn around and audit them. I have saved thousands of dollars by making time to hold outsourcing companies accountable.

BUILDING A DYNASTY

Our first company was a plumbing company turned construction company. We now have four companies. We have a nonprofit called MARS Community Development Corporation. The goal in starting this was to help the family and community. Another reason for this nonprofit was because we noticed a misappropriation of funds that we were giving to churches and other non-profits. When we saw how the money was being misused, we formed the non-profit. MARS Community Development Corporation enables us to be able to help our families and the community to build homes and enhance lives. The nonprofit now has a trade academy and is registered with the Department of Education, approved by the Department of Labor and is accredited by National Center for Construction Education and Resources (NCCR). The nonprofit has programs in carpentry, plumbing, heating, ventilation and air conditioning HVAC, cyber security, electrical, and farming. We have Brenda L. Hill, LLC, which is what I do my life and business coaching through. We also have Royal Dynastic Organics, LLC. Through this company, we grow, process and handle Hemp products on our farm in New Jersey. My trust is structured to form a dynasty. A trust is a vehicle that can outlive you and create income for future generations.

ADVICE TO ASPIRING ENTREPRENEURS

If you have had a burning desire to start your own business and you have a passion for it, then take that leap of faith and do it. Write down your goals and the vision of how you see your potential business thriving. Register your business name with your state first, get your IRS Employment Identification Number, open the business bank account, then take it one day at a time. Remember that success does not happen overnight, but you must sow your seeds by working hard, learn about the changes that are happening in your field, network, seek out mentors, research and do all you can do in a day. You will eventually see the fruit of your hard work. In the face of temporary defeat, do not give up. True entrepreneurs do not give up!

About the Author
Lanetta Bronté-Hall

Lanetta Bronté-Hall, MD, MPH, MSPH is a public health administrator, psychiatrist, and medical parasitologist. She is responsible for the strategic planning, scientific, and administrative oversight of the Foundation for Sickle Cell Disease Research (FSCDR). She is a leading national and international researcher and population healthscientist in the field of sickle cell disease, rare blood disorders, community-based research, andchronic disease management. Dr. Bronté-Hall has extensive experience in developing medical and research programs that are closely aligned with the recruitment and retention of underserved and underrepresented populations. She is President/CEO, of the Foundation for Sickle Cell Disease Research (FSCDR). She also holds the titles of Chief Health Officer (CHO), and Chief Research Officer for FSCDR.

Dr. Bronté-Hall received her Bachelor of Arts in Biology and Master of Science degree in Medical Parasitology and LaboratoryPractice from the University of North Carolina (UNC), Chapel Hill, Gillings School of Global Public Health. She received a jointDoctor of Medicine and Master of Public Health with specialization in Health Policy and Administration from the UNC Schools of Medicine and Public Health.

Dr. Bronté-Hall has served in leadership positions including the Chief Medical Officer of the Sickle Cell Disease Association of America, Sr. Medical Advisor to the CDC, National Institutes of Health (NIH), National Heart, Lung and Blood Institute (NHLBI) Advisory Council, and a member of the 2014 Expert Panel for the NIH, NHLBI for Sickle Cell Disease. She is married to Dr. Anthony Hall, a neurosurgeon and has a lovely daughter, Kyla Thorpe who serves as the COO.

Chapter 5

If it Doesn't Exist, Create it!

Lanetta Bronté-Hall

President & Chief Executive Officer

If you were to tell me thirty years ago that I would be an advocate for Sickle Cell Disease with a passion for finding a cure and helping those suffering from the disease, I would probably look at you with a long, blank, and puzzled stare. My desire after high school was to become a scientist. For this reason, I pursued a Master's degree in Medical Parasitology and Laboratory Practice after completing an undergraduate degree in Biology from the University of North Carolina at Chapel Hill (UNC-CH). While in graduate school at UNC-CH, I studied parasites and did research on African Trypanosome, giardia lamblia and other parasites such as Malaria. As I was conducting Malaria research, I ran across some information on the sickle cell trait and immunity to malaria infection, which interested me and aroused my curiosity. It was at that time, that I met a doctor who was conducting Bench research at the Duke University Comprehensive Sickle Cell Center. I became his graduate research assistant and was trained on laboratory techniques. Our research studied the defective release of tissue plasminogen activator in adults with sickle cell disease. As part of my training in a hemoglobin/sickle cell lab, I became a phlebotomist in the newborn screening unit. I performed Sickle Cell Screening on newborns and would prick the heels of babies as part of the national mandatory newborn screening program to determine if a baby had sickle cell disease or other diseases in newborns.

HIGH ASPIRATIONS

After completing an adult psychiatry residency, I immediately had my sights set on becoming a hospital administrator but was told that I needed to practice for at least 20 years before I would even be considered as an administrator. I was laughed at whenever I shared this desire. It was perplexing that I chose to become an administrator vs. starting a psychiatry practice. However, that was my desire, and regardless of what the norm was, I was going to pursue my goal. I kept running into roadblocks, so I called a few friends for advice. One friend introduced me to the former president of a popular university in South Florida who had many connections in the medical field. As I shared my desire of becoming a hospital administrator with him, he asked me how I could save the healthcare system some dollars. My answer to him was that the way to save money in healthcare is by practicing "quality healthcare" using evidence-based practices while monitoring, changing, and updating as needed. I told him that money follows quality. When we practice quality healthcare, the savings will come. Quality care should always be the ultimate goal of all healthcare providers.

As a result of my conversation with him, he connected me to the CEOs of two major hospitals. The first CEO I called granted me an interview, which was held in front of the entire executive staff of the hospital - all White men. While in the interview, I repeated my plan of how I could save money in healthcare. In that interview, I was asked, *"As a Psychiatrist, how would you know anything about saving money in healthcare?"* My answers were clear, concise, logical, and plausible, so the CEO connected me to the Director of Medical Affairs at this hospital. He was a retired surgeon. At the time, he was head of all the doctors at the hospital. After meeting with him, he said *"I will try anything for three months."* Needless-to-say, I was hired as the Medical Director of Clinical Resource Management on a three-month probationary period. This was a position never held before at that hospital and was created just for me, so I had to write my own job description. I ended up staying at that hospital for 10 years.

HIGH ASPIRATIONS ACHIEVED

As the Medical Director of Clinical Resource Management, I learned about policy and how hospital administration works. Since I am data-driven, I worked with the physicians, the chiefs of service, and the surgeons, asking questions, gathering data and conducting research for the purpose of developing protocols. Working on protocols gave me much insight as to how doctors were treating various conditions. In gathering data, I would ask the doctors, *"How do you treat congestive heart failure? How do you treat this? that? What is the first thing you do? etc."* I learned that they all were approaching conditions differently. The way that some doctors approached certain conditions was costly, but for others, not so much. Some doctors had patients with long hospital stays and others did not. I realized that there needed to be consistency and that each doctor needed to follow the same specific procedures for certain conditions they encountered; so I developed a protocol for when a patient came to the emergency room or was admitted, certain procedures were taken so that doctors did not overlook certain things.

Since I am action-oriented, I would read various research, then implement the evidenced-based protocols to see if they actually worked. While working on protocols and gathering data, I found out that physicians can be very stubborn. There were times when I had to show them that they did not order certain tests when they should have or thought they had. While talking to the physicians about these oversights, I was cognizant of the fact that I needed to be careful in how I presented and revealed information to them. Doctors do not want anyone telling them how to practice medicine. However, they were more receptive to me because I too was/am a physician like them, and I did not dictate to them what to do. Typically, hospital administrators are not physicians. More often than not, they are outside business people, which is why doctors feel a certain kind of way about hospital administrators trying to tell them what to do when they've not been to medical school. Being a physician in administration had particular unique benefits for me because I understood both the care side and the business side. As a result of my data-gathering research, I ended up developing about 20 evidenced-based protocols including, but not limited to Opioid detox, asthma protocols, surgical protocols, lung disorder protocols, heart protocols, pyloric stenosis protocols, and sickle cell disease.

DEPARTMENT OF SICKLE CELL SERVICES

While at Memorial, I started wondering what was going on with Sickle Cell, so I looked at the data and was disheartened at what I found. I found over a thousand Sickle Cell patients and lots of mismanagement. There were too many hospitalizations, the doctors did not like Sickle Cell patients coming to the Emergency Room so often, and many of the medical staff thought that the patients were drug users. Sickle cell disease is a blood disorder just like cancer is. Blood disorders are managed by hematologist-oncologists. However, few cancer doctors treat benign disorders like sickle cell and anemia. I began researching and reading literature reviews looking for evidence on how to manage this disorder. In the journal called 'Blood', a peer-reviewed medical journal published by the American Society of Hematology (also known as the Bible for Hematology), I found an article on a hospital in Bronx, New York where Sickle Cell patients are treated.

Dr. Lennette Benjamin, MD created a program where, instead of going to the emergency room, Sickle Cell patients go to a separate unit in the hospital to get their pain management and infusion therapy. Through this program, she kept patients out of the hospital, which ultimately resulted in substantial hospital savings. I wanted her protocols, so I emailed her, called her, and kept searching for her with no luck reaching her. I then saw on the National Institute of Health website that they were having a sickle cell scientific meeting that was opened to the public in Bethesda, Maryland, so I flew to the meeting. The doctors there were all academic doctors. There were a few brown people like me at the meeting, a handful of women, but mostly white men were there. As providence would have it, I ended up sitting right next to Dr. Lennette Benjamin. Needless to say, I was super excited to meet her. After a few conversations, I finally got her on a plane to Florida. She did end up giving me her protocols and they worked! After implementing her Sickle Cell acute pain protocols, the emergency room visits and hospital stays reduced by 80%! From that point forward, my mind became strongly focused on Sickle Cell as a result of this progress, so I presented the idea of totally replicating the program at Memorial to the CEO, CFO, and board of directors. It was a challenge at first because when I presented the data, they still were not initially on board. The CFO was concerned about payer reimbursement. However, one of the board members was impressed and saw the potential in the program. He asked the Executive team to assist me.

They reluctantly gave their approval. However, it was challenging trying to find a location in-house. I had approval, but nowhere to build. In the beginning, I could not find space in the hospital. Every ideal area I found was already spoken for. I came up with the idea of converting a patient room to a 4-chair infusion suite. Hospital real estate is always at prime. The previously identified locations would significantly generate revenue that a startup would not. I finally did not get push back on the real estate I settled on. I had it painted and had the beds taken out and lounge chairs put in. I just needed a doctor. Initially, I could not find one willing to see the patients but eventually, I found one who was willing to see the patients. A popup nurse's station was in the middle of the room flanked by two lounge chairs on each side. The room number was 519 and where Sickle Cell patients would go to when they came to the hospital.

By creating the Department of Sickle Cell Services, I switched the patients from the inpatient setting to an outpatient model, which reduced the number of emergency room visits and hospitalizations. After the first year, I made the hospital $1.1 million dollars. This savings augmented the fact that the ramifications of Sickle Cell patients not having to go to the emergency room is huge. I saved ICU,

ER and the hospital, significant dollars. On top of that, I continued saving them over a million dollars each year. I ran the Department of Sickle Cell Services for ten years. While at Memorial, I also applied for and received grants from the Health Resources and Services Administration and the Centers for Disease Control and Prevention. I brought the first sickle cell clinical trial to the hospital where we served as a clinical site for Duke University. As I knew the richness of including clinical research into clinical care, I sought a partnership that would get the Department established as an independent clinical research site. ...so I was bringing in money too.

While putting my efforts and energy into researching and collecting data on Sickle Cell at the hospital, I needed to figure out a way to get new education and new evidence out to the local providers. I figured that an effective way to be able to do that was to get them all together in one place at the same time. This could be done by inviting colleagues that the doctors knew and respected in their fields. Most of the physicians brought in were from hematology and oncology; so I created 'The Sickle Cell Disease Research and Educational Symposium' for the purpose of educating local providers about Sickle Cell Disease. The first year of the symposium was in Hollywood, Florida. I invited doctors from all over the United States to come and speak. They flew in from everywhere to attend. The Symposium is now an annual conference 15 years strong (as of this writing) and lasts three and a half days. Each year during the symposium, information on different content is provided, including, but not limited to psychosocial surgery, clinical translational science, basic science, clinical care, quality improvement, nursing, etc. An array of different speakers present information on various subjects. It is an annual event specifically centered around Sickle Cell Disease.

After ten years of running the Department of Sickle Cell Services at the hospital, they started

> *"I created 'The Sickle Cell Disease Research and Educational Symposium' for the purpose of educating local providers about Sickle Cell Disease."*

downsizing, and I was affected. However, the Sickle Cell Services was pretty much running on its own, so I was given a one-year severance package, which cleared the path for me to make my exit from the hospital to the University of Miami (UM) Miller School of Medicine. I had already been contacted by one of the doctors at UM who wanted me to be part of one of his grants a few years prior. I was not able to take advantage of that opportunity at the time because I was still full-time at the hospital. However, I could now bring my current CDC sickle cell surveillance grant over there. I had always wanted to work in academia, so my grant and I transitioned over to UM. I began teaching and conducting research in the Department of Public Health Sciences. I taught in the graduate, medical, and undergraduate basic science schools. While at UM, I began developing a registry for all Sickle Cell patients in the state of Florida. I wanted to do at UM what I did at Memorial, but it was so challenging and very difficult to do. There was lots of bureaucracy that prevented me from implementing the same program that I had set up at the hospital. It was disappointing for me not being able to set up a program for the Sickle Cell patients there.

FOUNDATION FOR SICKLE CELL DISEASE

I had a burden to do more for Sickle Cell patients, and I finally realized that although I had not initially chosen Sickle Cell, for some reason, it had chosen me and I knew I needed to do something; so I created a nonprofit organization called Florida Sickle Incorporated d/b/a Foundation for Sickle Cell Disease Research and immediately started looking for places to set up a FSCDR to run. I had no idea how I was going to run FSCDR, but I knew that a way would be made. Since I was still working at UM in Miami-Dade County while I was acquiring a FSCDR in Broward County, I met with my department chair and told him what I was doing. I told him about both the symposium and the foundation. When I explained that the foundation would cover 25% of my salary and effort, he was fine with it. Once that arrangement was approved, it gave me an opportunity to spend 25% of my time in Broward at the new FSCDR. I still had a year on my contract there, so for a whole year, I was running back and forth, but after my contract ended, I put all of my time, energy, and effort into the FSCDR.

After I officially opened the FSCDR, I called my former patients and informed them about it. The Sickle Cell community is a close-knit group, so the word got out fast. I began establishing my contracts with necessary health plans and physicians, and staff and was putting everything in place to be able to open by the timeline that I had given myself. Since I am not a provider, I had to make sure that the patients had access to one. I had kept good relationships with doctors; so I first contacted a friend who was a former Chief of Staff at the hospital where I had worked. I told him that I had set up a Sickle Cell Center in the community and that my patients needed a primary care provider. I asked him if I could contract with him to be their provider. He agreed. He comes over to see the patients on designated days during the week. I called another friend who is a Hematologist-Oncologist. He also agreed to start seeing the patients and he comes on designated days as well. After contracting with physicians, nurse practitioners, nurses, and hired staff was done, we had a grand opening and started providing services. I do exactly what I did at the hospital and even more! Ultimately two organizations were created. A non-profit, Florida Sickle Incorporated, d/b/a Foundation for Sickle Cell Disease Research which houses community grants, education, and social services and a for profit which houses the medical and clinical research practice Foundation for Sickle Cell Disease Research, LLC.

Sickle cell disease is a disease that requires a lot of care coordination and the patients must see many specialists, but doctors generally do not like to deal with the patients or their pain; nor do they like having to write so many pain prescriptions. The doctors essentially don't want to be bothered with Sickle Cell patients, so the bottom line is after the patients leave pediatric care, they are mistreated. I could not continue to stand seeing them mistreated anymore and God put it on "my" heart to do something, so I answered the call. Sickle Cell Disease is primarily seen as a Black person's disease, and as a result, Black people are mistreated. All over the United States, the patients have the same stories: nobody believes their pain, they are mistreated, they are disrespected, they are not assessed properly for signs and symptoms that they present, their pain is downplayed, they are treated as drug users, etc. Unfortunately, all of this centers around the social aspects of their disease. There are horror stories all over the country and for this reason, we need Sickle Cell centers all over the United States because one in 365 African Americans is born with Sickle Cell Disease. One in 12 African Americans carry the Sickle Cell Trait. One in 16,300 Hispanic Americans are born with Sickle Cell Disease and 100,000 Americans affected by Sickle Cell Disease.

At the Foundation for Sickle Cell Disease Research, we are more than a specialty practice. Patients come in for their welfare visits. They were so used to going in for pain only, that when they are not in pain, they ignore their necessary visits, so we had to get them to understand that certain things must be done every three or six months and that they needed to come in for regular visits. However, when they are in pain, we do treat them. We use opioids on site. While in pain, they sit in a lounge chair for hours and can get morphine, Demerol, Dilaudid, IV fluids, Zofran, Toradol and Benadryl. Every patient has their own unique pain protocol. We also have a medical marijuana physician, so we do everything we can to provide holistic care. For example, we know that opioids can also lead to organ damage. Sickle cell patients typically require significant high doses of opioids because of tolerance they have acquired from taking these medications since birth. Medical cannabis, CBD, CBG and other full spectrum hemp products help improve sleep, anxiety, pain and reduced opioid use.

SUPPORTING SICKLE CELL PATIENTS

At the FSCDR, we provide support so that patients can be seen by doctors who care for them and who understand the protocols, as well as the evidence. We set up care coordination, deliver quality, comprehensive treatment, and make sure that indicators are being met. We also work very closely with heath plan and hospital case managers. We have contracts with health care providers and participate in clinical trials with pharmaceutical companies since we do conduct clinical research on site. What we do has a positive impact on many other areas as well as the patients' system of care. I personally do everything from an administrative perspective, but with a medical touch. Being a physician in administration has afforded me knowledge that I otherwise would not have had. I have always written grants, so I continue writing grants for the center. I understand both the care side and the administration side. It's amazing how things all came together because at the outset, I had no master plan, but it just kept growing and building on its own. It is very rewarding when patients come in and make statements like, *"I am so glad that we have a place where we can come and not be judged or have people tell us that we come in too much. This place is a blessing!"* Some of the patients have said, *"We are so happy that we never have to go to the emergency room again. Nobody mistreats us here."*

This specific disease is a disease of oxygen deprivation. Every organ is deprived of oxygen and the patient has complications with all of their organs: their eyes, lungs, skin, liver, kidneys, urinary tract, uterus, penis, etc. Red blood cells carry oxygen to the body tissues, so if the red blood cell is sickled because of two genes that are sickled, the cell that is sickled cannot deliver oxygen to the organs and there is insidious oxygen deprivation, which causes excruciating pain and organ damage. If cells are deprived of oxygen for a long period, the organism cannot survive. If you have one gene that is sickled, you are protected against malaria.

ADVICE TO ASPIRING ENTREPRENEURS

My advice to you reader is that if you have a strong desire to start a business or a 501c3, do it! When preparing your plan, be sure to be able to answer these questions:

1. What is the vision for the business?
2. Who you are serving, who is your target audience?

3. Are you providing social services?
4. What is the mission of the business?
5. How do you plan on funding your business?

Sometimes you must step out on faith and do for your people what you know is right and figure out ways to make it happen. Become a collaborating partner in your community. For me, I knew that there had to be a better system for Sickle Cell, so I created it.

About the Author
Ericka J

 Ericka J was born and raised in Miami, Florida and matriculated in the Dade-County and Broward-County School System. She is a gifted hair stylist and owner/operator of Garden 7 Cosmetics in Savannah Georgia, where she currently resides. Ericka has created hair care products that are top of the line and used daily by trusted professionals.

Ericka embraced the gift that God gave her of doing hair at a young age, and she used that gift to branch out in other areas of beauty. Ericka has taught effective hair techniques to others to help them make money doing what they love, and she continues to help those in the beauty industry to hone their skills. When Ericka saw the need for a hair product that was simple, yet effective, she created it. She has since created several hair products that are sold all over the world. She also has her own brand of hair, wigs and a full line of skin products.

Her business, "Ericka" J is a common name in the beauty industry, known for quality and excellence. Ericka's products can be found at https://www.ErickaJProducts.com.

Chapter 6

When you see an Opportunity,
Capitalize on it!

Ericka J.

President/CEO

I f someone would have told me five years ago that at the age of 26, I would be a successful entrepreneur with my own product line, I would have probably believed them but also wonder HOW? At 21 years old I was not financially stable, was living in a new city, and had little to no resources. I never would have thought that a love for doing hair would catapult me to the level where I can make money while at home. When I find the time to sit down and resonate on how fast my business took off, I am amazed. My business name is, "Ericka J" and I am a successful entrepreneur in the beauty industry.

My entrepreneurship acumen started when I was in high school. I wanted a job so badly because all of my friends had jobs at either fast food places, supermarkets, the movies, etc. and I wanted my own money, but for some reason, I could not find a job. One day, I got my hair braided, but I did not like it, so I took out the entire front and redid it to my liking. When I went to school, a friend asked me who had done my hair. When I told her that I did, she asked me how much I would charge to do hers. When she went to school after I had done her hair, everyone complimented her and then they started asking me to do theirs. That is how and when I started doing hair for money and that became my job. I did not realize that styling hair was a God-given gift until the compliments started pouring in and the clients started lining up. From that point forward, I would spend my weekends doing hair. I was making good money - all while in high school. I was also baking cupcakes, then taking them to school and selling them. As I go back a bit farther, I can see how the gift of styling hair was in me before I even realized that it was my gift. Starting at the age of ten, I would go to the salon every two weeks, but during the weeks in between, I would experiment on my hair. I taught myself how to do it because I did not like the way my mom would do it. Whenever I did not like the way someone did my hair, I learned how to fix it myself. I would also practice different styles on my aunt.

A LESSON IN BUSINESS

When I was baking cupcakes and selling them in school, I would use my grandmother's supplies until the day that she told me that I needed to buy my own supplies. She said to me: *"That is not how business works. You have to buy your own inventory and not use other people's stuff to make money."* She told me to start using my own money to buy the products I needed because that is how business goes. …so I took some of my profits and bought eggs, cupcake mix, cupcake holders, etc. After I bought the supplies, I realized that I could not sell my cupcakes for $1.00, anymore because I would not make a profit after considering what I had spent on supplies. That was my first real lesson in business.

While in high school, I took a business class and learned about profits and losses. My business teacher chose three students at the end of the school year to go to Burger King Corporation and learn more about business. I was one of the three. He said that he chose us because he knew that we were serious about learning entrepreneurship. Burger King had a program where they taught students how business works behind the scenes. That is when I learned about writing a business plan, registering a business name, trademarking, etc. That was a really good experience for me, and the things that I learned are things that has helped me in my business today - especially the part about profits and losses.

After graduating high school, my mom told me that I had to go to college, but she wanted me to stay local before going off to school, so I enrolled at a local college. On the first day of class, the psychology teacher put on a documentary called, 'The Secret'. That was the day that changed the way that I think and approach things. If I never would have seen that documentary, I would not think the way that I do today and would not have had the confidence to accomplish what I have achieved up to this point. The documentary explains the universal law that governs all things and offers knowledge of how to intentionally create a successful life filled with peace, love, well-being, and abundance. However, college did not bring me joy. I felt a void while going everyday and I felt that I should be doing something else. Doing hair was what I loved. It brought me joy; so finally, I told my mom that I did not want to continue going to college, but that I wanted to pursue my love for styling hair. As a result, I enrolled in cosmetology school. Attending cosmetology school enlightened my understanding of the beauty industry and taught me so much. As a cosmetology student, I was able to learn a wide array of things, which really enhanced my ability to be able to perfect my skills. Not only did I learn the basics of hair dressing and styling, hair treatments, skincare and makeup, but I also learned about esthetics, skin conditions, health and safety, business practices and so much more. I also attended hair shows in different cities to learn what the new trends were in the beauty industry. I became really good at what I was doing, and I was fulfilled at learning about what I actually loved.

While still in school, my mom ended up getting me a job in a salon with one of her friends who had her own salon. While there, I worked really hard and was trying new things that I had learned about in cosmetology school. There were mostly older women who worked in the salon and I noticed how some were stuck in their ways and were not interested in venturing out to try new things in their profession. They did the same things day in and day out. As a millennial, whose mind was always on trying new things, I would tell them that they could make additional money by selling hair online or that they could teach hair classes. Some of them told me that they would not teach others their skills just for others to go out and make money from what they taught them. I was amazed at how closed-minded some of them were. It did not take me long to realize that trying to get them to think out-of-the box was an exercise in futility.

CAPITALIZING ON SOCIAL MEDIA

Instagram (IG) had been the new social media platform on the block when I was in the eleventh grade and I had created two pages. One was a hair page where I showcased styles and uploaded clips of how to do things, and the other was a personal page. During that time, people were not using their Instagram pages to promote their businesses, but I was using my page to showcase my hair styles while I worked at the salon. After I learned new things, I started posting them. As the years went by, I noticed that wigs and laces started becoming extremely popular, so I learned that technique and began posting wigs and laces. Wigs are one of the biggest things in the beauty industry today. People are always wearing wigs, installing wigs, and using products for styling/installing the wigs. I learned how to perfect every aspect of them and continued to post my work on social media. I did not care who viewed my posts or not. I kept posting and eventually started getting traction on my posts. I would make a lot of money at the salon, but then I would get tired for days at a time. I realized that in order to make more money, I had to go back to work and stand on my feet all day again. After a while, doing hair was hurting my back, feet, fingers, and hands. I started thinking that I did not want to go to work everyday to do hair in order to survive. I loved doing hair, but I felt that I should not have to overwhelm myself like that just to make money. It was not adding up the right way for me; so, a goal of mine then became how to make money while not having to do much work, so my mind went to work to figure out just how to do that.

TAKING HOLD OF OPPORTUNITY

The beauty industry is a billion-dollar industry and I was determined to make room for myself in the industry while also making an impact in the lives of others. I knew that I was very good at what I did, but I was not confident enough at the time to teach live classes, so at the age of 21, I created a YouTube channel and started uploading videos teaching people how to do things with hair on my channel. For example, I started off teaching how to install wigs or do braids. I didn't immediately start getting subscribers and lots of views. However, at the time I was the only person showing REAL hair techniques on YouTube. As others would only give half the information, I would teach from beginning to end. I then started getting contacted by stylists who were upset and asking me why I was teaching all of the techniques of installing wigs and that by me doing that, it will begin to take money out of their pockets because their clients will start doing their own hair. My response was, *"...you cannot service every person in the whole world."* When they saw how successful I became because of sharing my knowledge, they slowly began hosting classes of their own.

As time went on and I was consistent with uploading, people would write comments and ask lots of questions, most of which were about what products to use. I took advantage of the momentum, learned the internet, had a website developed, and created my own products to sell. My goal was to turn my viewers into my customers, so in 2017, I made my first product, which was an edge control. I was still doing hair and I would spend hundreds of dollars at a time buying different products for my customers because I did not know which ones were going to work for the styles that I was doing. I wanted a product that could be used for many different things, and I needed something simple. I would get five different edge controls to see which one would actually work. Some were too oily, some turned white after application and some were dry looking. That is why I created my own product. I talked to a chemist and explained my ideas. We then went from ideas, to samples, to trial and error, and finally to an actual formula.

> *"The beauty industry is a billion-dollar industry and I was determined to make room for myself in the industry while also making an impact in the lives of others."*

Since people were watching my videos, learning from them, and trusting that I knew what I was talking about, then I would provide an outlet where I was able to answer their questions while promoting my own products. After the edge control, I created three more products down the line in 2019. Since so many people were asking me to recommend wigs and hair, it only made sense that I created my own brand of hair. In trying to ensure that I chose a good brand of hair to sell, I tested out many vendors and many different types of hair. I would have my mom and friends help me test them out by wearing them for me. After a few weeks, they would tell me how they felt about their hair. I ran several different tests before choosing the right one and introducing it to the public. My clients would buy directly from me and it was convenient for them because I had everything they needed right there. After selling hair and edge control, I made a styling foam, a gel, and a wax stick that I currently sell on my website. Those were the main products that I released the first time around. All of the products are really good for natural hair and weaves. Whenever I uploaded a YouTube Video, I would showcase my products and add links to purchase them in the description box. That was how I was able to start making some real money. My products took off like a rocket and I was never able to keep inventory for long. When I first started uploading, I knew that my videos would get viewed, but I did not think it would happen so fast. I capitalized on the opportunity when I saw the handwriting on the wall. The orders were coming in faster than I could ship them out and I wasn't prepared for such an influx, so when I first started selling, my main focus was on fulfilling orders. In the year 2020, I sold two million dollars in products.

After the first product I launched, I began to rebrand my business. I learned about the simplicity of logos. When I looked at huge brands, I noticed that their logos were simple. Mine at the time was colorful, flamboyant, and blinged out with glitter, so I changed it to make it simple. I changed the colors from pink, black, white and silver to green. I designed my labels on my product with the same green, black, white and silver. I also changed the wording on my logo.

It had previously said, *"Hair by Ericka J"*. Had I left that as my logo, then that is all I would have been known for, so I took off the *"Hair by"* and my new logo simply says, *"Ericka J"*. It is simply a signature. Ericka J is what people know me by. That is my social media handle and it is ultimately my brand. My graphic designer suggested that I make the new logo a neon green color because it leaves an impression in the minds of people because I also drove a neon green Jeep Wrangler. People would tell me that whenever they saw that neon green color, they would immediately think of me. I was probably one of the only people in town with a neon green jeep. I was a walking brand.

LEGITIMIZING MY BUSINESS

I was not focused on legitimizing the business, but when it dawned on me that I had a bonafide business, I registered with the state of Georgia, got my IRS Employee Identification Number, and opened a business bank account. Currently, I am in the process of trademarking every name of my products because I don't want to risk anyone stealing my names. Social Media has played a huge part in the success of my business. I have kept my pages since high school and use them to leverage my business. I have had my IG page since 2011 and worked hard at gaining views and traction. Since I do not have a celebrity name, I had to work for my followers. To date, I have 264K subscribers on IG and 481K on YouTube. I am so glad that I took advantage of the internet. I used every social media platform to promote my business and it paid off tremendously. To date, I sell hair products and skin care.

When my confidence had elevated to a level where I strongly believed in myself, I began to teach classes. I taught how to install wigs because that was extremely popular and people wanted to know how to make them look natural, what glue to use and what products to use on them. When I taught in a group, where they only watched me, I charged $70.00 a person. When I considered what I would spend on supplies, booking the venue, and learning the value of my TIME, I increased the price. I was teaching a skill that could potentially make them up to $10,000 a week as stylists, so I then started charging $180 per person for a group class and the classes became very popular. I would also travel to different cities for group classes and I would cap the classes at 50 people per class. Some requested hands-on training, so I would open up a scheduler on my website and people would sign up for the classes that way. It was on a first come, first serve basis and the bookings would fill up quickly. It was only the client and me for the day. I charged $1,200 per person for private sessions. Everything is included in the private sessions including the wig products needed and the model. Clients would fly in or drive to me. I usually have about five sessions a week. When formulating my products, I worked with chemists and sampled many different formulas over time until I found the right formulas for what I wanted. I did not rush anything. Because of the education gained through cosmetology school, when I was testing products, I had actual knowledge about the chemicals and formulas. I knew what ingredients I wanted in my products and what I did not want in them. I did not want them to have a crunchy, flaky, or oily feel to them. I also wanted a natural shine, so I used every detail to create final products that would ultimately help me and other stylists when styling hair.

QUALITY FIRST

When I made my first product, I made my own labels because I didn't know any better. When trying to make things on your own, it oftentimes will fall below industry standards in terms of look, feel and quality. The good thing about chemists is that they have connections with companies that make bottles and do the labeling. After connecting with labeling companies, all I needed to do was come up with a design of how I wanted my label to look. The chemist also referred me to distributors and manufacturers. When your vision is big and you want the eyes of the masses on your products, you don't want your labels bleeding or falling off. I didn't want anything that looked cheap or cheesy. It costs money to produce an upscale product, but it is worth it to invest in quality because the first time you do something wrong or subpar and it becomes public knowledge, it will take a long time to repair your brand and your credibility. The internet can be very unforgiving. My product line took off so fast that I stopped doing hair because I could not do hair and manage the hundreds of orders that were coming in on a daily basis. There was no way to be able to do both.

Being able to make large amounts of money while not doing much work is a blessing. Work for me consists of packaging orders and driving to the post office to ship them off. It takes a lot of time to package hundreds of orders and is lots of work, but I would rather do that than stand on my feet all day, everyday doing hair. I still do hair, because it is what I love, but if I don't feel like doing it, I don't have to. I no longer style hair other than for family and close friends. I focus primarily on my product line. The lowest day of business sales has been about 100 orders in one day. The highest has been 4,000 orders in one day. When sales hit that high, it is usually when I decide to have a sale, which is not often. I don't have more than three sales a year, however. I usually have one on Black Friday and in the month of July because that is the anniversary of my product launch. It will be very hectic during that time, but it is the birthday of the business. When and if I have another sale, it will be on a whim. I may wake up and say, *"I think I will have a sale today"*. ...but again, that is not often. The reason why I do not have sales often is because when you always have sales, customers will always be expecting them. You will not make a good profit because people will get accustomed to not paying full price and then they won't value your brand as much, so I have random sales when no one is expecting them. Once the word gets out about the sales, all of my products sell out within a few hours. I have learned that when you have quality products that are effective, their popularity will spread like wildfire. I aim at providing quality products.

LESSONS LEARNED

In business, there will always be learning experiences. In 2020, I opened a store in Savannah, GA because I thought that was what I needed to do next in order to show progression. In my mind, that was the necessary next business step - from the house to the storefront. However, the storefront was not a good business move. Ninety-nine percent of my business comes from my website, so opening a store was not really necessary. After opening, I was not getting even ten customers a week. I still have the storefront, but it is not open to the public. Realistically, I need a warehouse and an office space, which is my next business move. My home, the garage, and the store are filled with boxes and getting a warehouse would be a smart business move because I need a large space to store inventory. Getting that storefront was a lesson learned, but I am still moving forward.

FUTURE ASPIRATIONS

My desire is for my products to be in Target and Walmart. I don't have them in beauty supply stores yet, but I want a much bigger brand. Discerning the right time to move is key - especially when in business. If you are not decisive and do not move quickly, you may just miss out on your opportunity. When I was getting so many questions about what products to use, what hair to buy, and how to do this and that after I uploaded my videos, I put myself in position to be able to steer customers to my own products. My videos were going viral and would get millions of views. As of this date, I currently have almost a half million subscribers on YouTube and millions of views. One of my videos has received 18 million views. I transitioned into a position where I was making money while staying home. I love doing hair, but I no longer *need* to do it to make money. I am no longer working for money. Money works for me. Whether I am asleep, awake or on vacation, I am making money because people are always watching my videos and always placing orders on my website.

ADVICE TO ASPIRING ENTREPRENEURS

Please understand that more often than not, it will not be your family or friends who will be a support for you. Do not let that discourage you. It will be complete strangers who will be supporting you. When I first started out, I would ask family and friends to like, support, and share my posts on social media, but very few of them did. Eventually, my mindset shifted, and I said to myself that I was going to continue to post whether people shared my posts or not. I stayed consistent. There were times when I would get sad or discouraged when I did not see my family and friends sharing or liking my posts, but they would share the posts of celebrities or buy and promote their products. I stopped worrying about that and continued to grind. If I continued worrying about who was not supporting me, I would not be able to see those who "were" supporting me, ...so I stopped focusing on the negative and began embracing the positive. The same people who were not supporting me in the beginning are the same people who, today act like they were there from the very beginning. I see them. People will not believe in you until they see the manifestation. Those are the people who I don't allow into my life anymore because if they couldn't support me when I didn't have anything to show for it, then they don't need to be around me now that I am living my dreams. I see people posting things like, *"If I start selling candy apples, would you buy them?"* Who cares if they will buy them or not! If that is what you want to do, then do it. If they want to buy it, they will buy it. If they don't, then someone will.

If you desire to branch out on your own to start your business doing something you love, then do it! When you believe in yourself, are willing to work hard, and teach yourself new things, you will begin to experience your dreams and aspirations come to fruition and it will be amazing. Believing in yourself will help you to realize that manifesting your goals is possible!

About the Author
Ann Marie Sorrell

Ann Marie Sorrell is an award-winning and accomplished business leader, global influencer, philanthropist, public speaker, and author. She is unwavering in her support of issues impacting women and minorities, economic development, and the environment.

Ann Marie is the president and CEO of The Mosaic Group, an award-winning advertising, marketing, and government relations firm serving clients throughout the US and the Caribbean for over 17 years. The firm has managed campaigns and projects ranging from as small as $10,000 to as much as to $3 Billion.

Ann Marie is also the President & Founder of Cannabiziac™. This global member-based company helps new and existing businesses capitlize on the rapidly growing $91 billion dollar industry by providing education, training, access to international industry experts, financial resources, networking events, mentorship, and advocacy. Cannabiziac™ offers on-demand courses, a cannabis-focused incubator and accelerator program, webinars, consulting and coaching services, and coworking spaces. Ann Marie also serves as an educator, consultant, and coach for Cannabiziac™.

Ann Marie was elected by 66% of Palm Beach County voters in November 2020 to serve as Supervisor for Palm Beach Soil & Water Conservation District, Seat 2. She has founded three empowerment initiatives: Black Girl Magic Global, Black Business Loop, and the National Black Economic Conference, which is held annually. She serves on several community boards and has won numerous awards for her leadership, business acumen, and community involvement.

Chapter 7

Starting a Business:
From Strategy to Execution

Ann Marie Sorrell

Founder/CEO, The Mosaic Group

T he Mosaic Group is a full service advertising, marketing, and public relations agency. We help companies, organizations and brands get the word out about their product, service, or initiative. We develop public awareness campaigns, assist companies in becoming more visible, increase their bottom lines or make the public aware of a social cause or issue. Our main headquarters is located in West Palm Beach and we also have offices in Broward and Miami-Dade Counties, Florida. We were conceptualized in 2004 but were established in 2005.

IN TRAINING

I learned about entrepreneurship through my mother at the age of 11. She sold shirts, food and Avon products to farm workers who would come up from the Caribbean to work with sugar cane. Every Saturday morning, we would get up early and drive to either Fort Lauderdale or Okeechobee Flea Market to purchase T-shirts, sweatshirts, or other long sleeve shirts that workers could purchase and work in. Each week, mom would give my two sisters, my brother, and I $30 each and told us to use our money to buy our own supply of shirts. We would sell our shirts alongside her for a profit. She told us that with the money made, we had to spend a portion to buy more shirts, put a portion in the piggy bank, and the leftover funds was for us to spend on whatever we wanted. We did that for about three to four years before they stopped the farm workers from coming up. I was also babysitting three children at $10 a head, and I also cleaned someone's office every Friday. At the age of eleven, I had three hustles and was making $150 every other weekend. I learned the value of work and the value of money at a young age.

THE BEGINNING

I started the Mosaic Group with $200, which was used for the Articles of Incorporation and the local business tax receipt. I had no money saved to start my business and just took a leap of faith. Not having any savings and starting a business was not the wisest idea. Prior to starting Mosaic Group, I had just finished graduate school with a master's degree in Business Administration and worked for a real estate developer as a sales and marketing representative. I was next in line for a significant promotion at the company to manage the sales of a 900-unit new construction project and was in the process of obtaining my real estate license per the request of the corporate team. However, I had a boss who didn't feel that I deserved the promotion because he believed that he should have become the sales manager of that property for which I was being promoted; so he created a false narrative about me and sabotaged my promotion. The last straw was when, on my only day off, I was called in to work, but I declined to work because my mom was ill, and I needed to take her to a doctor's appointment. I was told that I needed to find someone else to take her and that if I did not show up to work that day, I would be terminated. Needless-to-say, I took my mother to her doctor's appointment and I was terminated. Considering what was happening at the job with my boss and him not believing that I was deserving of the promotion, he used any means necessary to get rid of me so he could get the promotion.

After the firing, I made up my mind that I would become my own boss and not be subjected to answering to others while having them dictate to me what I could and could not do during personal emergencies - especially when it came to my mother. I wanted to be an entrepreneur and in preparing to start my own business, the first thing I did was evaluate what it was that I loved to do. I knew that I liked solving problems, so I started a management consulting company. However, after researching some of the largest corporate companies and the services they offered their clients, I quickly realized I had a lot of theoretical knowledge, but not enough practical knowledge or experience in management consulting. I reached out to a gentleman who owned a local management consulting firm to seek his advice, mentorship, and opportunity to work on a project with him. He did not have any client projects I could assist with at the time; however, he was in the process of restarting the Black Chamber of Commerce in my county and invited me to assist him. He told me that part of being a management consultant was helping businesses succeed, so he suggested that I volunteer to help so I could see what it took to start something from the ground up. He told me that although it would not be paid, it would be worthwhile, so I agreed.

Upon starting my management consulting business, I simultaneously started an event planning and marketing agency. Event planning was natural and fun for me. Unlike management consulting, I had lots of experience in coordinating and managing small and large events. I had been planning events since high school, starting with our first annual JROTC military ball followed by Junior Prom and other events. I actively planned events in college for all of the student organizations that I was involved in. I realized that my natural talent was creating experiences, handling logistics, interacting with people, and being innovative, coupled with my love for marketing, and so Upscale Events by Mosaic (dba The Mosaic Group) was born. The vision was to create a marketing agency that created unique, out-of-the-box experiences, was innovative, made a positive impact in the community, and was diverse in all aspects (people, industries, types of events and marketing campaigns, services

> *I realized that my natural talent was creating experiences, handling logistics, interacting with people, and being innovative*

provided, and more). My desire was to work with organizations ranging from small businesses to large corporations, with a niche for nonprofit entities.

My company's name is 'The Mosaic Group'. A mosaic is comprised of different shapes, sizes, and colors that are joined together to create a beautiful work of art. That is how I envisioned my company - a place where we would bring diversity, different people, places, events, innovations, ideas, and opportunities to create a beautiful work of art. When the TV show, 'The Apprentice' was out, it was my favorite show and I loved Kwame. He actually named their group 'Mosaic Company' and I looked at that as confirmation for me since that was my favorite show and Kwame was my favorite person.

TEAM FORMATION

My dream was big and ambitious, and I believed it would be great to collaborate with like-minded people on my new venture. I brought on three partners to join me. The first person I approached to partner with me was someone with whom I had served on a charity board with. At that time, she worked for a non-profit organization and invited me to become a charter member of the Young Professionals Network that she had formed. From there, we became friends and she supported me in whatever I did and always offered me valuable feedback. As a result, when I started Mosaic, I approached her about teaming up with me. And she agreed. Shortly after, I met a gentleman who did graphic design, website development, and video production. I shared my vision with him and brought him on as a partner. We also brought in an international speaker and corporate leadership consultant to partner with us from the perspective of connecting us with his client base. I did not require either partner to make a financial investment to be an equity partner, only their time and sweat equity. We had no contractual agreement in what was expected from each person. There was nothing contractual that outlined required time commitment, compensation, or when or how long their equity ownership would be vested. I quickly learned that was a big mistake! There needed to be a clear understanding of the partnership and each person's obligation and commitment. It is easy for people to not be totally vested into a business that is not their vision. Without a financial investment, they have nothing at stake to lose, so they may not be 100% dedicated to the mission and goals at hand. Unfortunately, two of the partners did not work out within the first year, and the third person stayed with me for ten years. For that period of time, we worked well together, built an amazing brand as a company and as individuals and survived one of the toughest recessions in American History. However, the time came when we had outgrown each other and our partnership. It was time to take our personal brands and goals to new heights. We amicably parted ways in the 11th year. Since 2016, I have led, managed, and grew my agency without partners. A valuable lesson that I learned is that if you are going to have business partners, you must be very clear about roles, responsibilities, contributions, commitments and expectations from the onset.

NETWORK OR NOT WORK!

Upon forming a new business, one of the first challenges is how to attract customers/clients. Since the inception of The Mosaic Group, I have attracted most of my clients primarily through referrals and word of mouth. I understood the value of developing a strong network early on. My initial clients came as a result of my volunteerism and relationships. I volunteered for the Urban League and served as the president of the Young Professionals Network and a member of the Urban League's Board of Directors. While volunteering to restart the local Black Chamber of Commerce, I was organizing networking events and chairing the membership committee. I also volunteered for a couple of youth organizations. Through my extensive volunteer work, I met many people in the community and they became familiar with my character and work ethic; so after starting The Mosaic Group, I reached out to some of those I served with and explained my new venture. People were eagerly willing to take a chance on me or confidently referred me to people they knew because of my track record and the spirit of excellence in which I operate.

My networking did not stop there; however, to increase awareness of the company's brand and services, I attended tons of networking events (breakfast meetings, cocktail receptions, dinners, galas, golf tournaments and more). I also invested financially in my networking efforts by joining chambers of commerce, professional associations, and other organizations where prospective clients frequent. I lived by the words of wisdom from one of my college professors: Network or Not Work! Building relationships was and still is a top priority for the growth of the business. People do business with who they know, like, and trust. Some of the keys to networking is to be intentional, bring value to the relationship (don't be a taker), and follow up and follow through.

MAKE SOMETHING OUT OF NOTHING

Starting a company with $200 is not an easy feat. There were no funds available for marketing materials, a website, an accountant or attorney, office space, etc. I had to be strategic and creative. I also had to learn a lot of new skills very quickly in order to not only service our clients but also manage our internal operations. I became a graphic designer, website developer, content writer, bookkeeper, operations manager, event manager, photographer, publicist, flyer canvasser, super networker, and more. I worked 18-20 hour days 7 days a week and got into the habit of getting no more than three hours of sleep a night. My motto "was no sleep til a million". I was willing to do whatever needed to be done in order to be viewed as a bonified, reputable company.

In the first full year of operations, we grossed about $75,000 which was great, and though chump change with four partners, it gave me the boost of confidence that 'The Mosaic Group' was on the road to success. In year two, business started to pick up and we were doing good. Clients were calling daily, and we were busy. Our calendar was booked with galas, golf tournaments, corporate and community events, press conferences, and more. We started getting more clients who needed public relations and marketing services. A couple of gentlemen who mentored me introduced our firm to the world of government contracting and infrastructure projects that required public outreach. We had developed a pipeline of more than $500,000 in projected revenues for that year.

That pipeline disappeared overnight with the great recession and the Bernie Madoff scandal. Nonprofit organizations that had their funding and endowments tied to Bernie Madoff's pyramid scheme abruptly cut off their consultants and canceled all of their fundraising events because they did not know where their money was going to come from. Ninety percent of our business was through charities and non-profit organizations. That was a substantial hit on the business and we saw our bottom line plummet. At the same time, with the great recession, government spending came to a halt because the government was focused on bailing out the banks, financial service companies, automotive companies, mortgage servicers, etc., so government spending on infrastructure stopped and many of the projects that our business had in the pipeline were infrastructure projects. We went from having half a million dollars' worth of work down to nothing. There was absolutely no money coming in and we had to get creative fast!

BUSINESS SURVIVAL

How do we survive this when no one is making or spending money? Unemployment was at an all-time high and businesses were shuttering around the country. I was determined to keep the business doors open and failure was not an option! We did what we did best, create events and experiences for people - but at an affordable rate (just enough for us to make a few dollars to survive and create the perception that our firm was thriving in the midst of a recession). We created win-win collaborations with various venues and organizations that needed exposure and access to people. We organized marketing and leadership conferences, created social events such as Meltdown Mondays (a weekly happy hour), Palm Beach Chic (invitation only exclusive weekly social), Fashion Shows, Exotic Car Shows, and more. We also created a weekly power networking breakfast where we charged $10 (we received $5.00 and the caterer got $5.00) every Thursday for people to come and network with others. We even created blinged-out Mosaic shirts to promote our brand (we wore them everywhere) and people wanted to purchase them. We were committed to survival!

Oftentimes, we only made enough to cover gas, but we did that for about three years. We got a few contracts here and there, but nothing major. However, we created such a good perception that our business was doing well in the midst of a recession that people were sending us their resumes wanting to come work for our company. Little did they know, we were barely making ends meet. From the outside, people were wondering how was it that we were the only company still surviving during the recession. It was because we were innovative and creative. We are in the business of creating positive images, perceptions and brands for others, so the time came when we had to do it for ourselves and we did a heck of a job! Had we not created a perception that our business was still being sustained and that we were still in good standing, we would not be in business today.

THE IMPORTANCE OF RELATIONSHIPS

During the times that we were putting on events, I invited a local commissioner to speak at one of my leadership conferences. After that day, she and I bonded and I ended up helping her with her election campaign for mayor. We held fundraisers for her, put together community events, knocked on doors, and made sure she was visible among Black voters and others. She won by a landslide, which was surprising to all because of the numerous candidates in the race. About seven months after she won, I sat down with her and asked her for advice regarding a few projects that I heard were being considered in the city. She contacted her procurement team and advised that my firm was a certified small business enterprise with their agency and was interested in learning about opportunities with upcoming projects. At the time, a developer was in the process of conducting interviews for a marketing and outreach team for a new $200 Million development that they were going to be building. We received a call from the developer's representative informing us that our name had come up and that they were going to be interviewing several firms and that they wanted to meet with us. During the meeting, we gave them an amazing plan of action. After the meeting, we were hired for two events. Those two events turned into four events, and I even convinced them to keep us on for the life of the construction project, which was two and a half years! …so a $25,000 project turned into a $250,000 opportunity. That was our comeback as a company! Had I given up during the recession or the Madoff Scandal, I never would have made it to that point in the business. That was in 2012. The project was completed in 2014, and it was as we were coming out of the recession.

NO MORE SCRAPS!

As a subcontractor, my colleagues would extend opportunities to me for my company to sub-contract with them when they won bids, and I was indeed appreciative. However, I started to realize that my company would do the bulk of the work but would only receive a very small piece of the pie. For example, we would receive about $7,500 for a $50,000 contract after having done the majority of the major work. When I finally understood what was happening, I said to myself that we were just as, if not more talented and skilled than those who were bidding as primes, but we were only getting scraps. Why were we not bidding as a prime? …and so I took a big leap of faith in 2014 and bidded on one of the largest marketing contracts in one of South Florida's municipalities and I was determined to bring my "A" game. I was not concerned about being the lowest bidder. I was focused on being the BEST bidder.

We received the notice on Thursday before Memorial Day informing us that we had been shortlisted. Out of ten firms, we had placed number six and were the only Black-owned firm. They wanted us to present to them on that Tuesday after Memorial Day, but my entire team had plans on going out of town since it was a three-day weekend. However, everyone scrapped their weekend plans. We ordered T-shirts and designed all sorts of things in preparation for the presentation. We were hell bent on going from number six to number one. We were the first company to present that morning with our boards, T-shirts, and presentations. The municipality was looking to rebrand three entire areas that were being redeveloped, so we offered to not only come up with a brand, but we presented a complete strategy for bringing the three communities together because there had been some racial tension. We presented a strategy for how we would brand the community as a place where residents could live, work, and play; a place for companies and developers to come and invest; a place for small businesses to grow and thrive; an ideal destination. We brought on an economic development consultant and a real-estate consultant that discussed how we were going to partner with the retail federation to bring more retail to the area. We also focused on the area that was predominately Black to make sure that it was not going to be gentrified and would maintain its rich heritage and culture. This was done in an effort to preserve its history.

As the only Black firm, we came from a perspective of understanding the importance of that particular area and surrounding neighborhoods with a goal of preserving their history. Our team brought a different perceptive that the city needed to hear while simultaneously letting them know that we would still work with both sides of the track. We ensured them that we could still bring everyone together while ensuring that all sides are able to sustain their identities, which are unique to them under the general brand. We came with concepts and a campaign called *"Forward Together"*. We convinced the selection committee that we could do that with the three neighborhoods; that we would break down the racial and social economic barriers and move this city *forward together*. They loved the concept, the thought process, and the creativity that we put into it. We left them all in awe. However, that did not mean that we would win the bid.

We were the highest bidder, but we brought an amazing plan, strategy, and concept, that by the time we finished the presentation, we went from number six to one of the top three. I was actually having lunch with one of my competitors when I found out that our firm had ranked number one. While we were eating, he congratulated me and told me that he had just received an email on his phone that my team had ranked number one. We went from number six to number one! We got the job and received a three-year contract. It was an amazing day! That was my first time bidding as a prime. I was no longer a subcontractor. Since then, I have only competed as a prime.

As a result of receiving such great reviews from several of our clients, we've received many referrals. People started calling us and wanting us to be on their teams. We then started doing work for governmental agencies throughout South Florida and across the State. Had I not stepped out on faith to bid as a prime, we would still be getting scraps. I believed in our abilities, expertise, creativity, and work quality. Needless-to-say, having faith paid off.

THERE IS ONLY PLAN A

There have been moments that I have considered giving up the business, but those were short-term thoughts. The recession during 2008-2011 was extremely challenging. Living off of approximately $7,000 a year was not easy. I lost my home to foreclosure during that time and was pretty much homeless - all while trying to run a business. While all of this was happening, my 14-year old niece was uprooted, abandoned, and placed in m y care. With nowhere to live and the uncertainty of how I was going to provide for myself financially, I asked her to trust that I would take care of both of us despite the dismal situation. At that point, I figured I would get a regular job, but no-one was hiring. I was able to get a job as an adjunct professor starting with one course, which helped to sustain me while creating events and holding on to the business.

A friend offered me a place to live that had been abandoned by one of his relatives. It needed a lot of work to make it livable, but we made the best of it for two years. I made just enough money for food, gas, essential items, and whatever was needed to keep the business going. It was a low point for me. I wanted to give up, but I kept a smile on my face and kept facing each new day with hopes that things would change. I had read a chapter in 'Think in Grow Rich' where they were digging for gold. They only needed to dig one more foot until they found the gold, but they gave up and left their equipment there. Someone came behind them, found their equipment, started digging in the same spot and found the gold. I told myself that there was no plan B or C - there was only plan A for The Mosaic Group to survive and thrive, and I only needed to metaphorically dig another foot.

ADVICE TO ASPIRING ENTREPRENEURS

I would like to encourage all who aspire to go into business for themselves, to pursue your dreams with your eyes wide open and approach your business endeavors with goals, plans, strategies and foundational components. Be able to answer the rudimentary questions and do the following things:

1.   **Ideation**
   - What is your why? What are you passionate about?
   - What do you love to do that you would do for free?
   - Is it viable and can it be monetized?

2.   **Visualization**
   - Do you have a clear vision of what your business looks like at a success level?
   - Write down your short-term and long-term goals for your company. Set action plans and timelines for each goal.
   - Create a business model and plan.

3.   **Action**
   - Figure out how much you will need to get started and develop a plan for getting the funds to start it.
   - Write down the steps that you will need to get the business up and running.

- Look for how you will capitalize on and monetize your business.

4. **Network**

Do not underestimate the power of networking. You must network or not work! Relationships are a two-way street. It is not just how you can benefit, but how you can add value to others. Faith and the law of attraction will give you what you are looking for, but you must be willing to also give of yourself.

5. **Sacrifice**

Be prepared to make sacrifices. You must understand that starting a business will require lots of hours and time away from loves ones. It requires long days and sleepless nights, financial risks, and physical, mental, and emotional stamina. You must be willing and ready to make the necessary sacrifices in order to reap the future rewards.

6. **Faith**

I cannot talk about faith enough. You must have a burning desire in your belly and belief in your heart, mind, and spirit that everything will work out even when things appear bleak in the natural. You must rely on your faith to get you through.

7. **The four "Rs"**

You must apply these in everything you do:

Relationships: It is not about who you know, but who knows you. People do business with those they know, like and trust. Relationships opens doors of opportunities.

Readiness: Don't get ready, stay ready.
Preparation and Planning + Opportunity = Success.

Resilience: Be ready to bounce back regardless of what obstacles you face.

Relentless: Focus, be intentional and consistent and keep moving forward despite what happens around you.

Starting your own business can be extremely rewarding. When you are destined to be your own boss, you will never be satisfied working for someone else. If the thought of your own business has been on your mind for quite a while now, then you may want to put yourself in a position to do it. My advice is to write down your goals first. Set up your business name with your state and get your IRS business tax identification number. Decide if you will work from home or rent out space. Research your industry and find out what is happening in the industry today. Look at those who are at the top of their game in your field and ask yourself how you can stand out and be unique in your field. Seek out mentors who can give you sound advice. Save your funds, so when you are ready to really step out on faith, you can sustain yourself. Decide if you want partners, and if so, require them to invest financially in the business to ensure their commitment to the success of the business. Lastly, put it in the Source's Hands and trust the process of the Universe. Little becomes much, when you think it, feel it, believe it, and let the Source work!

About the Author
Ann McNeill

Ann McNeill is the first Black female contractor in the State of Florida. She is the Founder/President of MCO Construction & Services, Inc. and MCO Consulting, Inc. She is also the founder of 'Think and Grow Rich International Mastermind Association', Inc. and The National Association of Black Women in Construction (NABWIC).

With over 40 years' experience in the construction industry, Ann speaks professionally, both nationally and internationally and travels the country sharing and imparting her knowledge. She is a proud Rotarian, a graduate of Florida Memorial University and a member of Delta Sigma Theta Sorority, Incorporated.

Ann McNeill speaks and coaches nationally, teaching work-life balance principles. She has impacted the lives of countless people with examples from her own life experiences. She encourages other to pursue endeavors that will change their lives by following basic principles, espoused by Think and Grow Rich.

Ann enjoys being the mother two beautiful daughters, Danelle McNeill-Tate and Ionnie McNeill, as well as the proud grandmother of Malachi Munroe and Rajah-Nia Tate. Mrs. McNeill is happily married to her "boyfriend", her husband, Daniel McNeill.

Chapter 8

Thriving as a Woman in a Male-Dominated Industry

Ann McNeill

Founding President, MCO Construction

W hen you are destined as an entrepreneur, it is in your blood. When you begin to realize that you were created to be a business owner, you may not know what that business is at first. In your quest to find out where you belong in the entrepreneurial arena, you may try many different things and you will have some failures, lose large amounts of money, and experience great disappointments, but with determination and persistence, you will find your niche; you will find where you fit; and you will find that thing that has been waiting for you to claim it. Until such time however, you must try as hard as you can to be wise and listen to that inner small voice that leads and guides you. It is called your intuition. Many people call it "women's intuition", but not only women have it. Men have it as well. When we refuse to listen to that still small voice, God, in His grace and mercy will send someone to warn us of impending dangers and/or failures.

SEEDS PLANTED

I started MCO Construction in 1982, almost 40 years ago (as of this writing) in Miami, Florida. As a woman in a predominately male industry, it has not always been easy. It was my husband who planted the seed for me to start a construction company. As we were relaxing and talking one day in 1979, he said this to me: *"If I had to do it all over again, I would not go to college. I would start a construction company."* My husband's words resonated with me because I had always wanted to start my own business. During this time, my husband and I were already investing in real-estate. We owned our house, a house across the street, a duplex down the street, and one around the corner. When repairs were needed in our properties, we would go to the local library and conduct research on how to do the repairs and then would fix them ourselves. As we continued to read and do research, we discovered that construction workers made more money in an hour than we made in a day, and they sometimes made more in a day than we made in a week. It was at that time that I decided to go to trade school to study and learn about how to build houses. I learned all about construction and needless-to-say, was the only woman in the classes. In those classes at trade school, I learned how to do most of the trades. I also learned that I could hire workers as subcontractors in all the trades that were required. I also learned that many people who know the trades, did not know the business, and many who knew the business, did not necessarily know the trades. For me, although I had learned the trade side, I had not learned the operation side of a construction company.

PREPARATION & TRAINING

Shortly after finishing trade school, the Miami race Riot happened in 1980 following the acquittal of four police officers in the death of Arthur McDuffie. After the riots, I came to Miami to help with the rebuilding because they were looking for contractors. As I would meet various Black contractors at those meetings, I would ask if they needed volunteers. Business owners were glad to have a free laborer and I was more than happy to volunteer so I could continue learning. Since I had learned so much in trade school, I had no problem doing roofing, carpentry, ordering materials, digging trenches, doing roofing, dry wall, painting, or helping with paperwork, etc. However, I did not have the application for connecting the book knowledge to the field knowledge. I volunteered for about three years and it proved to be extremely beneficial because I learned so much. I also found out about the work habits of others. I would observe how folks would get paid on Friday, then not come to work on Saturday. This was because oftentimes, the companies would take any able body who needed some quick money to work. Finding good workers was a challenge for most construction companies. While volunteering, I would continue going to the meetings to find out about any updates. While at one of those meetings one day, I found out that Mr. Thacker, from Thacker Construction was looking for someone to manage his construction office. I jumped at the opportunity to work for him because I thought in my mind that I could learn how to manage a construction company under him. While working for him, I learned everything I could. I became his protégé and he became my mentor. From the onset, I told Mr. Thacker that I eventually wanted my own construction company, but that I did not know about the operational side of it. Working with him would give me the experience I needed and teach me the things I needed to know about the business side. While working at Thacker Construction, I began studying for my contractor's license.

MCO CONSTRUCTION

Eventually, I started MCO Construction, but under someone else's license. However, I was still working as an office manager for Thacker Construction. I had read Think & Grow Rich, which made a deep impact on me, and I was motivated more than ever to start my business. I had learned under Mr. Thacker that I needed to have a technical certification. Additionally, he told me that I needed to get a good estimator, a good CPA, a good banker, a good lawyer, and a good bonding company. The first bonding company was referred to me by the county. Coincidentally, the company they referred me to was the company that had given Mr. Thacker his first bond. They respected him, his business acumen, and they had a high regard for him, so when they found out that I had worked for him, and as a result of their respect for him, they backed me more than the average small business, which enabled me to go after projects under $500,000, but over $200,00. Because of this, I did not have the competition that other small businesses had because other Black contractors were not able to bond over a certain amount. They were able to go after projects under $200,000 because anything under $200,000 did not need to be bonded, but they faced challenges with getting bonded for anything over that amount. Since I had the backing of the bond company, I was going after contracts left and right, and was actually getting them.

I had my business while continuing to work for Mr. Thacker and I did not stop working for Thacker Construction until Mr. Thacker died years later. After that, my only job was working at my own business, MCO Construction. After Mr. Thacker passed away, his business closed, and I never worked for anyone else ever again. I had no choice but to put my heart, mind, and soul into my own business. After four years, my company was able to double the salary that I was making at Thacker Construction. I had learned from my mentor that I needed a really good estimator - someone who gives you an estimate of how much it will cost to do the work, and I had a good one who knew all the loopholes. My estimator taught me how to look for projects by going to the county, which had public bids because legally, they had to advertise. Back then, everything was all on paper, so I would find projects, bid on them, and would win most of them.

BUSINESS OBSTACLES

Owning a business was not always easy and I ran into some hard times. There were obstacles, but my commitment to my team, my clients, and myself is what kept me in business for so many years. There were days that I did not have enough cash flow, but there were always creative ways to overcome those cash flow challenges. One creative way was to ask the owners to pay me in advance. Another creative way was to ask for checks payable to both parties - to me and whoever I owed. That would guarantee payment for them. Doing this can also help with not needing a bond. The reason for a bond is to ensure that the people will get paid. Success in construction was realized as a result of more than hard work. The principles that I had learned from *Think and Grow Rich* were followed diligently. The other contribution to success was accountability that was reinforced through the process of masterminding. I founded the International Mastermind Association, starting with one group and expanding to groups all over the country. Accountability, the key to setting and reaching goals, is provided through the process of masterminding.

I am also the founder of *National Association of Black Women in Construction* (NABWIC). I created a place for black women and girls at all levels to connect in order to build a pipeline into the industry. This was a way of passing on my success. The association was created for four subgroups:

1. Black girls in junior high school, high school and college. They could see themselves through us as entrepreneurs, architects, lawyers, contractors, laborers, small business people, and other trades.

2. Black women in professions throughout corporate America. They control procurement and construction contract opportunities.

3. Black Women in the public sector: cities, counties, states, and school boards. They control procurement opportunities.

4. Black Business Women: business owners, those in the trades working as architects, engineers, and contractors.

Using the principles of Think and Grow Rich as a foundation, I have been able to create success not just for myself but for so many others. That has been and is still my vision. Closely following the principles of TGR has empowered me to build lives, families, and communities. As a master builder, it my goal to build stronger and better lives. You can do the same. Step out on faith and just do it!

Every year in business you should take time to review, receive, replenish, restore, reassess and then relax. Many of us spend more time and money planning our relaxing time for our vacation than we do planning our business time. Take time right now and do an assessment and a professional review of your business life. If you have ever read the book 'Acres of Diamonds' by Russell Cromwell, then you know that some of the finest gem stones in business are in your own backyard; but you will only discover them if you take the time to review, receive, replenish, reassess, and restore your business. Begin now, to set the goals to take small steps to improve the quality of your business. Start with the short-term goals for the next three to six months. Then you can look out at one year to five years, then to ten.

ADVICE TO ASPIRING ENTREPRENEURS

To date, I can truly say that the greatest sale I have ever made as a business person was the day I personally bought what I was selling. This was the day I saw the big picture. That was the day I truly began believing what I was doing to help my clients. When starting your business, make sure that your vision is crystal clear to you. Having a clear purpose is essential and makes it easier to embrace the business idea that God has given you. It is very sad that there are men and women who think they have failed when they don't succeed. Failure is only temporary and if you are able to look beyond the temporary defeat and forge ahead in spite of obstacles, you will eventually experience the success from your hard work. However, if you give up after temporary defeat, you will never discover the success that awaits you just around the corner. Don't give up!

About the Author
Dr. Venessa Walker

Dr. Venessa Walker, affectionately known as "Dr. V" is a Chiropractic Physician, Minister of the gospel, and educator. Dr. Walker is the founder and owner of Walker Chiropractic and Wellness Center. She is also the creative mind behind 'MyHolBody', supplement and wellness brand, where she sells vitamins, supplements, and other daily immune support for the body through her website. She has over 19 years' experience in the chiropractic field and over 12 as a Chiropractic Physician with advanced training in sports, personal injury, and prenatal.

After graduating high school from a Medical Magnet Program, Dr. Walker earned a Bachelors of Bio-Medical Science degree from the University of South Florida and her Doctorate of Chiropractic from Palmer College of Chiropractic. She is the co-author of, *Getting Well: Mind, Body and Spirit. A Guide to Healing and Healthy Living in Every Area of Your Life*". She currently travels internationally empowering individuals through her program, 'Transform YOUR Life' and encourages individuals to make their health a priority - which aids in accomplishing greatness. She is on a mission to help her patients reach optimal health through chiropractic care and lifestyle changes.

Dr. Walker is the President of Broward County Chiropractic Society and President of the Owen Walker Jr. Foundation, Inc. (501c3). She is a member of Countyline Worship Center Church of God and a member of The Fort Lauderdale (FL) chapter of The Links, Inc. She sits on the Board of the Broward Regional Health Planning Council and is also a graduate of Leadership Broward, Class 33. Dr. Walker has received numerous accolades and recognitions, both locally and nationally and she continues to mentor young African American women.

Chapter 9

Stepping out on Faith and Starting my Business!

Dr. Venessa Walker

Founding/CEO Walker
Chiropractic & Wellness Center

Starting your own business is like having a child. When you get the child, you want to make sure it is healthy, fed, constantly nurtured, receives regular checkups, is clean, and looks presentable. Regardless of what happens, you must have a mindset that despite circumstances, you will continue to care for that child until it is able to care for itself. No different with a business. When I decided to take that leap of faith to start my own business, I founded Walker Chiropractic & Wellness Center. After graduating from Palmer Chiropractic School in 2007, I immediately established a business under my name. I have always had an entrepreneurial spirit in me, and I knew that at some point in the future, I would have a business; so I incorporated my business name and secured an EIN number, but did nothing with it for a few years. There was something in me that told me that when the time came, I would need it.

I became interested in the field of chiropractic when I was an undergrad student at the University of South Florida in Tampa. During my freshman year in college, one of our class assignments was to shadow someone who was working in a profession that you desired to be in. My thoughts at the time was to pursue becoming a sports physician, so I looked in the phone book for someone in that field who would allow me to shadow them. After finding someone, he thoroughly answered all of my interview questions, and it was at the end of the interview when he revealed to me that he was actually a Chiropractor. I was shocked because I did not know that a Chiropractor could also have a specialty in sports. He did basically all of the same things I desired sports to do. My interest was then peaked. After the interview, I sent the doctor a thank-you note, and in response to my thank-you note, he offered me a job. That started my journey towards becoming a Chiropractor. I worked for him all through undergrad school, and it was while working for him that I decided that I too wanted to be a chiropractor. Dr. Jones became my mentor and we are still in communication this very day.

After finishing undergrad, I immediately went to graduate school at Palmer Chiropractic College of Florida. Unfortunately, after graduating and returning home, my 22-year-old brother Owen, passed away from a heart-attack and I fell into a depression. I took some time off and then went to work for another Chiropractor. This time, I was working as a Chiropractor Physician. I was the only Chiropractor in that office because the doctor/owner who had worked out of the office had moved to another state. While working at someone else's office, there were limitations of what I was able to do. The office that I worked in only cared for accident patients who had experienced some type of soft tissue/spinal trauma. They did not provide general Chiropractic care and they did not take general insurance. I did not have the latitude to treat the patients the way I really wanted to, but I saw the potential to provide them with so much more than what we were providing. I wanted to be able to see patients with different types of Chiropractic needs and not only focus on one segment of patients. A fire was lit under me, so I asked if I could provide other services for the patients, but the office wasn't equipped for that. The field of Chiropractic is on a three-tier prong. The focus should be on looking to remove subluxation in the spine that may be caused by thoughts, trauma and toxins. The focus at this particular office was only on the trauma. However, there is a large segment of people who have the thoughts and the toxins that need to be addressed. I wanted to be able to treat those patients as well. I felt stifled; and the creativity and desire in me to do more for patients were crying to be manifested. Unfortunately, I had to suppress them until such time as I was able to release them.

It was while working at that office that I embraced the concept of opening up my own Chiropractic office. The desire in me to open my own practice so that I could provide care to various subgroups of patients grew stronger. I did not know how or when I was going to do it, but I knew that I was going to have my own practice. It was just a matter of when. It had gotten to the point to where this desire was on my mind both when I woke up in the mornings and when I went to bed at night. I started writing down my goals, attaching action plans to those goals, creating timelines for each goal, and I regularly met with my Mastermind group to help keep me accountable. In life, timing is everything, so after two years of working in that office, I opened up my own practice. When the time came to take that leap of faith, I contacted a realtor to help me find a location. I knew that I wanted to be in Miramar (Florida) because I wanted to serve the community in which I had been raised and that had given so much to me. I needed to give back to my very own community.

As God's providence would have it, my mentor in Tampa who I had worked for in undergrad was retiring and getting rid of everything in his office. When he called me, it was during the time that I was stepping out on faith to start my own practice, so the timing could not have been better. At the time, I thought that I would probably get a few things and perhaps be able to furnish maybe one room at my practice, but I was able to furnish the entire office! I took EVERYTHING in his office - equipment, chairs, massage tables, adjustment chairs, office furniture, a printer, tables, pictures for the walls

> *"I did not know how or when I was going to do it, but I knew that I was going to have my own practice. It was just a matter of when."*

and even a shredder - all for a blessed price! My father rented a U-haul and drove to Tampa with some brothers from church and they brought everything back. A friend came to the office and added some creative decorating to the lobby, church members made a desk for me, and others pitched in to help in various capacities. I had lots of support. It was all divine timing. I learned that when you step out in the right time, everything will fall into place. God had navigated the circumstances for me to get my training for four years while I was in undergrad working for someone who taught me the ropes and showed me the way. I was a good steward during my training and learned all I could. I was dependable, responsible and loyal. As I look back, I also understand now that working for the second chiropractor revealed my passion for wanting to do more for patients. I was able to see what it looked like and what it felt like to not be able to express the desires, gifts and skills that God has given you. Working there gave me a clear vision for what I wanted to provide for my own patients when able to do so. I am grateful for both experiences. Both taught me valuable lessons. When it is God's will, you must follow His leading. When God puts purpose in us, that purpose must be fulfilled, but again - timing is everything. There must be a season of training and learning. You cannot step out before the appointed time. There must be a season of training and tutelage. God will always send someone to prepare you, and during that season of learning, you must absorb all you can. That person could be a mentor or coach, but God will never give you a vision without making a way for you to get the proper training. When you are ready, God will let you know through signs, and things will fall into place.

FUNDING MY BUSINESS

I did not get a business loan to start the business, nor did I even consider getting one. I used my own funds. All I had was God's guidance, my family's support, and lots of prayer. I used the last bit of my savings to make a down payment on an X-ray machine. I did not have a manual on what to do, but I knew what I had seen, learned, experienced and done in previous offices, so combined with my education, experiences, and qualifications, plus the things that I wanted to do for my patients, things just fell into place. After opening the business, I started networking even harder. I made sure I was visible. Prior to opening the office, I had been heavily involved in my community, showing up at events and serving when needed. I had been part of the local chamber of commerce, the urban league young professionals' network, I would sponsor teacher appreciation at some of the local schools, participate in career day, and I became the "go-to" Chiropractor for the local high school. I would meet many people at health fairs, community events, networking events, church events, etc. All that proved to help me tremendously in getting the word out about the business.

There were times that the fear of failure would try to creep in, but I did my best to overcome it by thinking positively. I spoke with a female Chiropractor colleague who shared with me that when she opened her office, all she had was a table and $2,000 to her name, but she made it happen. After hearing that, it significantly decreased any fear that I might have had. Once I made the decision to really do it, there was no turning back. I went full speed ahead. It was not a coincidence that when I decided to finally step out on faith to open my own practice, that my mentor was retiring and called me to come and take everything in his office. That was divine timing. There are no coincidences in God!

In 2014, I had a grand opening for Walker Chiropractic & Wellness Center, and it was beautiful. Since I had been so plugged into the community, people fr om everywhere came - family, friends, classmates, church members, associates, and elected officials from multiple counties. There was a ribbing-cutting ceremony, hor d'oeuvres, and networking. It was a beautiful day! After the grand-opening, the time came for me to get down to business. There were many, many sleepless nights because I had to make sure that paperwork was in

"I was able to see what it looked like and what it felt like to not be able to express the desires, gifts and skills that God has given you. It is not a good feeling."

order, permits were in order, insurance documents were correct, etc. but again, - it all fell into place because the timing was right. In the beginning, I was not only the doctor, but the secretary, the custodian, the accountant, the bookkeeper and the assistant. That is how it usually is at first. You are everything until you are able to hire people. I understood that and rolled with the punches. I wanted patients to be comfortable when they came to my office, so I would be there late at night cleaning and making sure that things were in order. Attention to detail was a priority for me. Today, there are five people on my team: two chiropractic physicians, two chiropractic assistants, and one chiropractic physician assistant.

At Walker Chiropractic & Wellness Center, we treat infants, children, teenagers, adolescents, adults and the elderly. Basically, we see patients from neonate to geriatric or as they say, "from the womb to almost in the tomb." In our office, patients are given a neuro spinal scan to see what their body is telling us. We look to decrease nerve interference. It is very important to make sure that the autonomic nervous system is stimulated. The focus is to decrease the interference in the nervous system. We do not only do adjustments in the office, but we diagnose, nurture patients through care, and make sure that they are getting quality chiropractic care.

GROWING PAINS

There were some growing pains, a few obstacles and some disappointments, but my team and I got through them. In the city where my practice is located, physicians are required to have a special license in order to have an X-ray machine in their office. I did not know that and received a fine from the city. After three years in business, I got myself a business coach because I had spoken with a chiropractor colleague who told me that as a result of hiring a business coach, his monthly revenue doubled, so I secured the same coach. Prior to the coach, I had already been looking for a larger space, but one that I could own. My coach also encouraged me to expand because as the number of patients increased, the office space became too small to accommodate them, leading to longer wait times. I could not find anything in the city to own and I wanted to remain in my city. However, there was an empty space directly next door to my office for rent, so I ended up acquiring that space and expanding right next door. More growing pains emerged while seeking to expand. Waiting for permits was frustrating and I continued to flush out dollars for various unexpected expenditures. An initial $10,000 six-month expansion project turned into an over $100,000 two-year project. Needless to say, I was extremely frustrated, but my team and I got through that obstacle as well.

After the Covid pandemic, I had a substantial decrease in revenue due to patients staying home, afraid to come out, and/or quarantined; but I had an increase in overhead. The expansion, which was finally finished served to be a blessing because we were able to space the patients out for social distancing purposes. It also contributed to decreased wait time due to more available rooms and enabled more adjustments of patients at a time because of the space. The expansion being completed when social distancing was mandatory was also divine timing.

REDIRECTION

As of today (July, 2021) I have been in business for seven years, but I started to redirect my focus. I desired to help my healthcare community on another level, through coaching, mastermind and mentorship. I want other female healthcare providers like myself to know that, their dreams are possible. I may the decision to hire two associates. They are amazing African American female licensed chiropractors. Hiring them has freed me up to do other things and gives me room to breathe, since I now am not seeing every patient that comes through the door. I focus more on the CEO aspect of the business and overseeing the total operation as opposed to having to treat every patient. I am now able to provide the coaching guidance that allowed me to accelerate to other female healthcare practitioners through, Healthcare Mavens in Business.

THE IMPORTANCE OF CHIROPRACTOR CARE

I love what I do. Without a doubt, it is my calling, but quiet as it's kept, a chiropractor wears many hats. My mom would often tell me that I chose a profession where I have to use both my brain and my body. A chiropractor's job is definitely a physical one. People tend to underestimate chiropractic care, but the truth is that you must incorporate it into your annual checkup regiment. On an annual basis, most people see their primary care physicians, their eye doctors, dentists; women see their gynecologists, etc. but rarely do we consider that the chiropractor should be added to that annual list of physicians as well. There are only about 8-10% of people under chiropractic care. Preventive chiropractor care is just as important as the others. You only have one spine and just as you get a checkup on your eyes, your teeth, and other areas of your body, you should want to get a checkup on your spine as well, so that you can know what is going on underneath it. When there is an underlying issue, pain is one of the last things to manifest. You don't wait until you have a toothache to go to the dentist, do you? In like manner, you should not wait until your back hurts to see what is going on with your spine. Pain is not an indicator. Pain is a symptom of the body saying, "I have had a problem for a while." Check your spine. Don't wait until something is wrong before you see your chiropractor. One of my biggest joys is seeing lives transformed through chiropractic care. Success for me is when patients report that their pain has significantly reduced and that they feel good!

ADVICE TO POTENTIAL BUSINESS OWNERS

If you have been flirting with the idea of starting your own business, then my advice to you is to be passionate about what it is that you want to do and make the preparations. You must lay the foundation for your business by setting goals, making a blueprint for how you want it to look, do your research, make some calls, ask the right questions, get your business name, EIN number and open the business bank account. Make sure your business is something that you love. Do not go into it just for the money because you will not be fulfilled. If you start a business because it is something that you love to do, the money will follow. Seek guidance. Don't totally rely on your own knowledge. There is so much that you do not know. Although you may know a lot, you do not know everything, so seek wise counsel. Proverbs 11:14 tells us, *Where no counsel is, the people fall: but in the multitude of counsellors there is safety.* It is also written in Proverbs 15:22 that, *Without counsel purposes are disappointed: but in the multitude of counsellors they are established,* so seek counsel. A business coach can take you very far. Write down your goals and desires. Whatever it is that you see in your head concerning your business, write it down. Make a plan of action for how each of your goals will be established and set realistic expectations. Do as much as you need to do in a day and take it one day at a time. Don't be anxious but focus on what you can do today and leave tomorrow for tomorrow. Never give up. In the face of adversity or disappointments, take the lead and continue moving forward. Whatever disappointments you face are not there to remain. They will pass and they will leave a lesson behind. In the face of fear, never give up! God has not given you a spirit of fear. Face your fears and keep moving forward. …And lastly, be patient. Success does not happen overnight. I am routing for you!

About the Author
Thema Campbell

Thema Campbell is the visionary, founder and CEO of Girl Power Rocks, a non-profit organization aimed at providing services for young girls who have been traditionally referred to as "at risk". Thema has renamed these young ladies "at-promise" girls because in her eyes and in the eyes of her team, these young ladies are amazing and filled with promise. Presently, their bright futures may be in danger of abuse or self-harm, so Girl Power Rocks provides them with help, protection, and guidance.

Thema works tirelessly to spread the word about the needs that many young girls from underserved, underresourced and disenfranchised communities have. She is constantly advocating for funding and policy changes in order to continue providing much needed services for such young ladies. Under Thema's leadership, Girl Power Rocks has formed partnerships with agencies to help further their mission and provide support and services to numerous young girls and their families. Girl Power has become a community staple in the Liberty City and Overtown Communities of Miami, Florida, and continues to build on their success of providing trauma-focused gender specific services throughout Miami-Dade County.

Thema was presented with the Miami-Dade County Bar Association "Women of Distinction - Community Champion Award" and was presented with the 2021 Small Non-profit of the Year Award from the Miami-Dade Chamber of Commerce.

Chapter 10

Out of Your Heart and Into Your Hands!

Thema Campbell

Founding President/CEO
Girl Power Rocks, Inc.

Because of a little voice that kept whispering in my ear, I knew at a very young age that there was something that I was supposed to be doing with children. I just did not know exactly what it was. Prior to starting Girl Power, I helped to co-found 'Concerned African Women' with my sister-friends. Starting that organization was a wonderful, but challenging undertaking. It was something that I thought at the time was my calling. It was there when I realized that children trusted and opened up to me. They told me their deepest secrets, some of which I wished I had never known. They felt safe with me, especially the girls. I came to believe that God had revealed my mission and had equally empowered me with the passion and desire to carry out this thing in my heart that was focused on helping children. It still was not clear what that thing was at the time. What I did not know however, was that where I currently was, was not where I was supposed to end up. It was puzzling to me because what was there not to love about Concerned African Women? I was working with two of my best friends, I was young with lots of energy, a beautiful single mother of three and very happy. However, things started to take a turn for the worse and I finally decided to walk away from the organization that I

[105]

had cofounded and worked so hard at for ten years. I left with nothing to show for my ten years of hard work and sacrifices, other than time lost with my own children while taking care of other people's children. I also received no severance pay. I just took my purse, left the building, and have never looked back. My ego kept telling me that I was crazy to walk away with nothing and to turn around quickly before it was too late to go back, but the whisper in my ear kept saying that what was waiting for me was ahead, not behind, so I kept walking. Where to? I did not know at the time.

CUTTING THE CORD

After leaving Concerned African Women (CAW), I fell on some hard times. I had not been smart with my finances and had used up all my savings, so I knew that I had to do something quick, fast, and in a hurry. During this time, my daughter, the last child at home was graduating from high school and about to go off to college. She had no idea of the stress I was under. After she left for college, I fell into a deep state of depression and started second guessing my decision to leave CAW. With no money coming in and too proud to ask family and friends for help, I eventually lost my townhouse in Miami Lakes, Florida and moved to an apartment in North Bay Village, which turned out to be my saving grace. Riding back and forth over the bridge was sort of a metaphor for washing away negative things, letting go of the past, and embracing my future.

Although I was starting from scratch (again), I was back on track with a new sense of urgency. The voice that had been a soft whisper in my ear was much louder now, but the message was still the same. The children need you. I began to slowly embrace the voice in my head and as I did, my purpose became clear and was eventually crystalized. Things started to move quickly, so I reached out to a friend and mentor who had his own nonprofit called World Literacy Crusade. My purpose for calling him was to ask for his support and guidance in starting my own nonprofit organization. At the time, I did not even have a name for it. As we talked, I shared with him that I had a vision to help and serve children. He informed me that he was not doing anything with his nonprofit, and that I could have his. He literally gave his nonprofit organization to me, and we began operating under the name of, 'World Literacy Crusade of Florida, Inc.' I took this as a sign that I was on the right track. Things were starting to line up. I was super elated and extremely grateful. My sister-friend who had worked with me at CAW had also resigned, so together we started working on building the nonprofit. We immediately went into operation mode and started trying to secure a location where we knew children needed our services desperately. That place at the time turned out to be the City of Opa-Locka, Florida.

We shared our vision with the City Manager at the time, who loved and embraced our concept. He told us that our services were much needed in that community and welcomed us with open arms. He then offered us a location to operate, free of charge. The multipurpose room was in Opa-Locka's library and had not been used in years. There was old furniture pushed up against walls and the room was extremely dusty. Neither my partner nor I were strangers to hard work, so we started cleaning, dusting, and painting. After the room was ready for use, we promoted the program throughout the neighborhood and started recruiting. Children had already been coming to the adjacent library, so we would recruit students by talking to them and their parents right there. Many apartment buildings surrounded the area, so we began talking to parents in the neighborhood and got permission for their children to come to the program. Unfortunately, and with great disappointment, less than one year later, we found ourselves in need of another place to operate. We had officially made the decision to segue into gender specific programs for girls and so 'Girl Power' was born.

GIRL POWER ROCKS

We needed a stable place to operate, so I reached out to a friend and community icon who offered to sub-lease us office space in Liberty City at a reasonable cost. We jumped at the opportunity. Moving to Liberty City, Florida had its ups and downs with plenty of slumlords to go around. Liberty City is home to one of the largest concentrations of African Americans in the county. In the 1940s and 1950s, the city thrived as a middle-income African American community serving as home to prominent figures and thriving businesses. The city even had a Black-owned hotel. An interstate construction, easements and restrictive covenants altered the neighborhood. Increasing numbers of families that lived below the poverty level migrated to Liberty City after their displacement from nearby communities. This transformed Liberty City into a blighted, low-income community, which led to the flight of middle to higher-income African Americans out of the area. Crime went up and the Liberty City community went down. This made way for slumlords to move in managing their properties with the least possible investment and adopting it as a business model. However, Liberty City was good for Girl Power because we had an opportunity to anchor ourselves in the midst of a community that needed us the most.

Not only were we serving girls during after school hours, but we also formed partnerships with the local school district and began offering 'Alternative to Suspension' programs to girls who were serving two or more days of outdoor school suspensions. The more girls we served, the more we discovered that a large population of those young ladies were victims of one or more forms of trauma and/or abuse, ranging from sexual assault to incest, to all other forms of abuse. We also discovered just how resilient girls are. We also formed partnerships with agencies to provide mental health services to them and their families, which is now a core component of Girl Power's programs and services. Starting Girl Power has been a blessing, not just for the girls and their families, but also for me as the President/CEO. That voice whispering in my ear and that thing that had been in my heart was now "*IN MY HANDS*". As I would reminisce from time to time about what happened at CAW and what happened in Opa-Locka, I realized that all those transitions had made me even more determined and had fueled my passion to carry out the work I had been called to do.

Just when my pace had slowed down a bit and things were running very well, my partner decided that she was leaving Girl

Power. This was a devastating blow to my ego and heart. She was not only the other half of Girl Power, but she was also my friend who was like a sister to me. I swallowed that hard pill although it hurt me deeply and I sent her off with love. Our friendship and sisterhood went far beyond Girl Power and has endured to this day. What I knew for sure was that the show must go on. The seeds had been planted, nurtured, cultivated, and grown into a beautiful tree that continues to bring forth fruit in the lives of so many young girls.

Operating Girl Power has not always been easy. One of the major obstacles that all non-profits constantly face is getting people to understand just how much trouble our girls are in today. The Delores Barr Weaver Policy Center 2019 Report on the Status of Girls' Well-Being in Florida reported that: *One in ten girls reported being forced to have sexual intercourse; Sex trafficking of children in Florida is prevalent. In 2018, there were 1,521 investigations into victims of commercial sexual exploitation that resulted in 400 victims being verified (the majority are female)."* The literature shows that the average age of recruiting girls to be bought and sold for sex is 13 years old. Between January 2018 and February 2019, 7,581 girls were removed from their homes due to physical abuse, sexual abuse, domestic violence, or parental drug abuse. More than one in three girls experience depression; one in five girls report thinking seriously of attempting suicide.

Many girls we serve are no strangers to the traumas described above. We never know who will walk through our Girl Power doors, so the staff and I understand the utmost need for high and regular doses of love, patience, understanding, support, protection and guidance. At one time in Girl Power's history, we unconsciously viewed the plight of the girls we served through lenses that did not validate who they were. The term "at-risk" had been widely used and accepted. None of us considered that the connotation was negatively impacting our children even further. We replaced the term "at-risk" with the term "at-promise" to support and validate girls and empower people that work on their behalf to see them in a more positive light.

FUNDRAISING AND FUNDERS

Operating a non-profit requires that we constantly create new revenue streams and exciting, unique ways to fundraise. Having a board that has your back can never be taken for granted because fundraising is where the board should really come in. Girl Power has two major fundraisers each year, one being our annual brunch that features Girl Power's very own Girls' Choir of Miami. The event attracts a large and diverse audience of donors and supporters who love good music, good food and moving and grooving to amazing gospel, jazz, and secular music performed by our girls' choir and invited music guests. Delectable food is also served. Our other fundraiser is a Day Party held late in the afternoon. It is called a "Party with a Purpose". Donors pay an entrance fee to listen to great music by our favorite DJ who plays the kind of music that everyone loves. We also sell T-shirts and raffle off items. Although the Day Party does not raise as much as the brunch, the event is still lots of fun and does raise money. The bar is always open, and the dance floor is always full.

Girl Power has become a community anchor in the Liberty City and Overtown communities and continues to build on the success of providing trauma focused gender specific programs and services in the South Dade communities. We are humble and grateful to receive the support of several city and county funders. Our community partners are just as important to Girl Power as our funders are. Community partners help the organization to make ends meet by providing services to our girls and their families that we otherwise could not afford. When you are doing something that has a positive impact on people and your service is being rendered from the heart, God will send the resources you need. Staying focused on your goals and mission and being good stewards of the money, goods, and services entrusted to you is part of what it takes to keep your agency afloat and thriving.

"AT PROMISE" GIRLS

What is an at-promise girl? She is an amazing and promising young girl whose bright future is in danger of abuse or self-harm and who needs help, protection, and guidance. Getting funders and policy makers to recognize and invest in "at-promise" girls has always been a major challenge. What I have come to know over these past twenty years working in the field is that this is a special population that needs immediate attention and protection. The more we talk and not act, the more girls are lost to the streets, to the school to prison pipeline, to human trafficking, and to a life of poverty for herself and her off-spring.

Policy changes that specifically benefit at-promise girls seem to be a difficult concept to wrap one's head around - especially if they came from a loving, nurturing, protected childhood. Not all girls are fortunate enough to grow up in such a loving household; and if you are one of the fortunate ones, it may be difficult without judgement and victim blaming, to understand the plight of those who were not so blessed. Women are the first teachers of men and women and we must invest heavily in those first teachers. My work and our work as a community, is to raise our voices and roar if we must to do whatever it takes to put an end to the trauma and abuses that stifle the hopes and dreams of at-promise girls. For years, I had focused so much on ensuring that the organization stayed afloat that I did not devote much time to advocating for policies that support at-promise girls. The voice is still whispering in my ear and I am listening. The Florida Girls Initiative brings together thought leaders, researchers, policy makers, funders, and data keepers together to help chart a plan of action in order to keep at-promise girls safe and to protect their bright futures from harm and danger.

INTO MY HANDS

Knowing that I hold the trust of so many people and knowing how much they depend on me to do the right things, keeps the pressure on. Every time I hear or see for myself one of our success stories, the pressure fades to black. Witnessing the fruit of hard work and labor, reminds me each time of why I do what I do. When a former Girl Power student calls me and says, *"Ms. Thema, guess what? I got accepted into FAMU!"* …it warms my heart because I know from whence she came. …or when I hear, *"Ms. Thema, I am coming home for the summer. May I come work at Girl Power? …*it warms my heart because I know from whence she came. When they say to me, *"Ms. Thema, I am getting married and I want you to come to my wedding"*, …it warms my heart because I know from whence she came. However, not all of the stories have happy endings. Sadly, over the years, we have lost some girls to the streets and a few have even passed away. Despite those, we must keep moving forward, but we do remember them all, especially those who suffered abuse, neglect, and woes of society. Those unfortunately were beyond our reach. Some of the girls suffer great tragedies that are far beyond what a young girl should ever have to experience. Supporting them through their experiences has left many scars on my heart that serve as a motivator and reminder of the work that is still ahead. There are those who we will never forget, even if we wanted to, because of the indelible impact of their stories.

There was one young girl whom I will call Kujichagulia (the third principle of Kwanza), because she had so much determination. Her mother lived in another country while she lived in Miami with her father, several siblings, and other relatives. Kujichagulia was neglected, unkempt, had bad hygiene, could not communicate well and was reading far below her grade level. Despite all her challenges, she showed up for programming every day. She was basically raising herself and taking care of her siblings the best she knew how because her father worked all the time. We matched her with a mentor through our Sister Circle Mentoring Program and began to see a slight increase in her behavior and grades. One day as we arrived to work early in the morning, she was sitting on the steps of Girl Power waiting. We found out that on her 18th birthday, while she

> *Supporting the girls their experiences has left many scars on my heart that serve as a motivator and reminder of the work that is still ahead.*

was still in high school, her father told her that she had to leave his house because he was no longer required to take care of her because she was considered an adult according to the law. Through her devastation and having no place else to go, she turned to Girl Power for help. After hearing her tell me her story, it sounded hard to believe, so I called her father. He confirmed what she had told me. After getting over my initial outrage, I begged and pleaded with him not to abandon her and to allow her to return home until she at least finished high school, but he refused to take her back. Although I was enraged with her father, there was a part of me that understood his plight. I had to realize that he too was a victim of ignorance, poverty, and trauma.

The staff and I immediately got to work calling family members and agencies, but to no avail. Finally, I called her Girl Power mentor and after she spoke about the situation with her husband, they both agreed to take her in. Even though they took great care of her, Kujichagulia carried deep emotional baggage and was spiritually broken. Like most young girls with similar stories, she went looking for love in all the wrong places, eventually getting pregnant. Despite this, her mentor embraced her even more and created a loving and permanent home for both mother and child. That was over ten years ago and the bond between them is still strong to this day. There are many Kujichagulia stories inside the walls of Girl Power. We exist because girls need us to be there for them despite their circumstances and mistakes. We love them by dishing out heavy doses of love, support, guidance, protection and understanding.

MAMA HATTIE'S HOUSE

Now in my sixties, there is no second guessing myself or looking for validation from others. I have now become the change that I want to see in the world. My validation comes from my Creator who provided me with plenty of help and guidance along the way starting with my own mother and my grandmother. I will always remember my mother saying, *"You don't know how you gonna leave this world or who you may need, so be nice to people and show respect to everyone."*

My grandmother, affectionately known as Mama Hattie was someone whose house was always filled with love, laughter and people; and there was always food (leftovers) on the stove. Growing up, her house looked huge but after becoming an adult, I often wondered how on earth had that small home loomed so big in my memories. Mama Hattie was a small woman but in my childhood memories she was a large figure, but in actuality she weighed one hundred pounds soaking wet. The answer finally came to me. Her love and caring loomed large over our entire large family. Everyone who knew her, loved her. Mama Hattie's house was where we always wanted to be. During the summers we picked blackberries, peaches, plums and muscadines. Blackberry and peach cobblers were staple on Mama Hattie's dinner table. Mama Hattie had a huge impact on my life. She influenced me in ways that I could never imagine growing up.

IN HER HONOR

In Mama Hattie's honor, I am now in the process of building a home for girls who are going through challenging transitions in their lives. The building will affectionately be known as 'Mama Hattie's House'. Seeing how she had a hand in raising so many of us grand and great grandchildren, nieces, nephews, cousins and friends, it is only befitting that I honor her memory and legacy. Preliminary designs envision Mama Hattie's House as a five story, 34,000 square foot facility, located in the heart of Miami's Overtown community, and slated for construction (as of this writing) by the year 2023. The complex will be situated on a 30,000 square foot parcel of land conveyed by Miami-Dade County. Mama Hattie's House will be surrounded by environmentally friendly landscaping that provides girls an oasis, along with solar-powered energy and a rooftop garden. It will offer a residence for girls aging out of foster care, exiting detention, or transiting from homelessness, abuse and neglect. Programs under the same roof will provide physical, emotional, social, academic and career support with an emphasis on preparing young girls to lead fulfilling and productive lives. Girls will also have access to on-call medical and mental health services, and a host of on-site support services. The facility will also house residential co-living style space, house parent quarters with full amenities, common area spaces for dining, studying, social gatherings, music, and artistic explorations, a commercial kitchen space where girls can learn to cook healthy meals and make Mama Hattie's blackberry and peach cobblers.

Mama Hattie was a woman of few words. She taught by example while taking care of so many women, children, and men too. She was not short on love or discipline and had hedges in the front yard where you had to pick your own switch if you needed some discipline. We all (sisters, brothers, cousins, and strangers) loved being at Mama Hattie's house because we believed she could do anything and could make anything from scratch. Even though Mama and Mama Hattie have both been passed on for many years, I still miss the homemade biscuits and blackberry and peach pies made from fruits picked right off the tree. I came to understand that Mama Hattie was the first female entrepreneur that I knew. On Mondays through Fridays, the working women would drop off their uncooked food along with their pots and pans for Mama Hattie to cook for them. On their way home from work, they would pick up their home cooked food for their families and would pay Mama Hattie for her services on Friday when they got paid. Mama Hattie also cooked what I know now as delicacies for the local white people in Sparta such as turtles and snakes. We had no medical or hospital insurance, so Mama Hattie had a remedy, plant or herb for any sickness known to man. Mama Hattie, who had less than a third-grade education, was a healer and the smartest woman I have ever known.

ADVICE TO THOSE WHO WISH TO START A NON-PROFIT

When people ask me if they should start a non-for-profit, my recommendation is always to look for a nonprofit that is already providing the type of services you have in mind, join them, or offer to open another chapter someplace else where the services are needed. However, if you are determined to start your own, do it to help people. Nonprofits are the backbone of society when it comes to helping others and serving the community. Many people in communities need help for a variety of different reasons, and the government cannot do it all. That is where nonprofits step in. Nonprofits provide help and support to the people who are suffering in our communities; thereby increasing the quality of their lives and making this world better for all of us. If you do not desire to start a nonprofit in order to help others, then you are in it for the wrong reason. Nonprofit work is a thankless job. For those who desire constant praise and accolades, the nonprofit sector is not for them. Additionally, money and resources DO NOT come knocking on the door. You must be strategic in going after those dollars. You cannot be discouraged when you hear the word no. Your passion and commitment should keep you in hot pursuit of dollars and resources in order to keep your non-profit afloat. The competition for nonprofit dollars is fierce and shrewd. You must know where the money is and go get it, otherwise, you will be out of business FAST. If your dream is to do for others more than you do for yourself, you are right where you are supposed to be, and let me be the first to welcome you to the rewarding and wonderful world of nonprofits!

About the Author
Burnadette Norris-Weeks

Burnadette Norris-Weeks is a Partner in the law office of Austin Pamies Norris Weeks Powell, PLLC. She serves as counsel to various governmental entities, including cities in Broward, Miami-Dade and Palm Beach counties. She represented the Broward County Supervisor of Elections Office for more than sixteen years as its General Counsel. The law firm also handles serious personal injury and wrongful death cases throughout the State of Florida.

Burnadette is the founder of the Women of Color Empowerment Institute, Inc. (WOCEI), a membership organization with the mission to enhance and expand leadership opportunities for women of color. In addition to other programming, WOCEI spearheads a yearly conference that brings together hundreds of women in leadership from across the country.

Burnadette is active with various boards and community organizations. She serves on the Board of Directors for the Greater Fort Lauderdale Chamber of Commerce and the Board of Directors for Habitat for Humanity of Broward. She is a graduate of Leadership Florida and of Leadership Broward. She also serves as a member of the Southern District of Florida's Federal Judicial Nominating Conference.

Burnadette's extensive community and professional involvement has earned her the Above and Beyond Award from the American Bar Association's Section of Litigation; the Urban League's Margaret Roach Humanitarian Award and a Lifetime Achievement Award from the T.J. Reddick Bar Association. She is a past honoree of the National Trumpet Awards Foundation and was recognized by Legacy Magazine as one of South Florida's 25 Most Influential and Prominent Black Women in Business.

Burnadette is admitted to practice law before the 11th Circuit Court of Appeals and the United States District Courts for the Northern, Middle and Southern Districts of Florida. Her law firm was recognized by US Business News as the "Legal Elite Litigation Firm of the Year for 2020".

Chapter 11
Running Profitable Businesses

Burnadette Norris-Weeks, Esq.

Partner Austin Pamies Norris Weeks Powell, PLLC

I know that it sounds cliché, but if there is something that you've always wanted to do, don't give up. Planting small seeds in your brain and taking moments to jot down your dreams are foundational strategies for making dreams come true.

Before I ever ran a business, I *saw* myself running a profitable business. I've sporadically journaled for many years and when I go back and look at goals that were set years ago, it is astounding how closely those goals align with my current reality. A portion of my childhood was spent in Cocoa, Florida. In the mid to late 70's the local Sheriff's Office had a community program called Junior Deputies. One of our field trips was a trip to the Brevard County Courthouse to see what goes on in courtroom proceedings. I was about nine when we took the trip and other than the television show Perry Mason, it was the first time I'd seen the inside of a real courtroom. I vividly recall seeing a judge and others in the room who appeared to be prosecutors, public defenders and witnesses. While our group sat on the hard-wooden benches and watched the courtroom activities, I instinctively knew that I would be a lawyer one day. That short trip to the courthouse planted a small seed in my memory that grew over time and allowed me to dream.

Another influence in my business trajectory of owing a profitable law firm included seeing another Black woman own a successful firm at an early age. She was the mother of a childhood friend and her name is Pearl Crosby Smith. I always felt a sense of empowerment whenever I had an opportunity to be around Ms. Crosby Smith. She was admitted to the Florida Bar in 1973 and, at the time, was one of the only Black women practicing law in the State of Florida. She had her own law practice and owned her own building. In my eyes, she was a BOSS! It wasn't until years later that I made the connection that seeing Ms. Crosby Smith, a woman with such grace and style, played a role in helping me to see that I also possessed the grit, gumption and faith needed to start a business. At a young age, I was fortunate to see someone who looked like me conquer goals and make their dreams a reality. Ms. Crosby Smith practiced law for nearly 50 years before voluntarily taking inactive status with the Florida Bar. She is now retired and living in Georgia.

In college, from the beginning, my goal was to go to law school. I started as a business major but after realizing that one of the classes that I dropped (because I could not decipher the professor's accent) would only be offered again the semester *after* my regular graduation date, my double major of Criminology (pre-law as I called it) quickly became my only major at the University of South Florida. I was determined to take the LSAT exam in time to start law school in the Fall of 1988 and that is what I did. I was fortunate to graduate from college at a time when universities really cared about diversity and inclusion. Because my LSAT scores and grades were good, there were many scholarship opportunities available to me. I recall meeting with a recruiter from the University of Iowa and being told that the university could pay me over $20,000 a year to come to their law school. Being a Florida girl all of my life, the thought of temperatures less than 70 degrees on a regular basis was simply not appealing for any amount of money. I eventually chose the Florida State College of Law over numerous other schools in and outside of Florida. The school not only offered financial assistance, but their brochures emphasized smaller classroom sizes. I was extremely nervous about law school and felt that smaller classes would be good for me. As it turned out, my law school class was the largest class accepted in the history of the school. By the second year of law, I was anxious to figure out how all of the legal concepts learned in the classroom applied to real life. In short, it was time for some practical experience. I interviewed for an internship with a firm called Knowles & Randolph, PA (K&R). They were a Black-owned firm in the downtown area of Tallahassee within walking distance from the Florida legislature. The firm operated out of a beautiful two-story renovated house that appeared to have been built in the early 1900s. As soon as I walked into the building for the interview, it felt like a place that I could stay for a while.

I was fortunate to start my legal career with K&R, a boutique law firm representing governmental entities, corporations, and handling serious personal injury matters. It is the identical type of work that my current firm has been handling for many years. Outside of the occasional secretarial bickering, from which I stayed clear, that firm was a foundation for watching top-notch professionals do what they loved to do while also maintaining community involvement. Their formula for success was to keep their heads down and get the work done. Their successful partnership has survived four decades. I was employed by the firm for approximately five years after graduating from law school. My plan upon leaving K&R was to start my own firm. I even had a friend who was in a leadership role with a major union organization who offered me free office space right next to the Florida Capitol Building. I initially agreed, but my uncertainty as to whether I was ready to start my own law firm led me to take an offer to serve a dual role of Staff Attorney and Staff Director for a Select Committee at the Florida Legislature. One year later, I moved to South Florida with plans to marry my now husband of more than 22 years.

The beauty of the law profession is that every day presents an opportunity to solve a problem and help someone improve their life. Whether it is helping someone recover damages for injuries sustained in an automobile accident or writing language for an ordinance that will help to improve an entire community, lawyers help people every day. I do not believe that it is necessary to do what you love in order for your business to be profitable, but it certainly helps.

A couple of years before leaving Tallahassee, I was voted President of the Tallahassee Barristers Association. I loved the work and found that it was easy for me to pull people together to get things done. I already knew many of the movers and shakers in Tallahassee through working with a respected firm, but stepping into this role helped me to bring independent value to the law firm and solidify my own relationships with local lawyers and judges. At one time, the Governor's Office reached out to a firm partner asking whether I wanted to be appointed by then Governor Lawton Childs to a County Judgeship. My immediate answer was a resounding "No", as I could not imagine such a restrictive life that would require avoiding a camera if someone saw you with a glass of wine.

After moving to South Florida in 1997, I had a few connections in the South Florida area who were mostly people that I knew from the National Bar Association, from college or from my sorority. I had already learned the value of community engagement in business and in the back of my mind still had plans to open my own firm. The entrepreneurial seeds from observing Attorney Crosby Smith and the attorneys at Knowles and Randolph had already been firmly planted in my brain. It was just a matter of time before I stepped out. There is always a need for lawyers who care about the community to serve on boards and I was asked frequently to get involved. As a result, I quickly made new friends as well as rekindled old relationships with folks from college and law school.

> *"The beauty of the law profession is that every day presents an opportunity to solve a problem and help someone improve their life."*

Through relationships, I was quickly offered a job at a state agency working in the civil litigation department. The work was enjoyable, but when one of the secretaries showed me the distribution list indicating the large number of cases that were assigned to me compared to other attorneys in the office who had been practicing for about the same amount of time, I started looking for other opportunities. I not only felt used, but I also felt underpaid. It was clear that my years at K&R had better prepared me for litigation work. I was winning trials and taking on the work load of three attorneys all at the same time.

So many women of color stop practicing law in search of more fulfilling work. In that regard, many attorneys get to a point in their careers, usually at year seven or eight, where they feel stuck and encumbered. I suppose the same can be said of other professions, but at this time in my career I thought, *"Is this all?"* At the same time, I was performing well as a professional, but wanted more for my life besides billing hours and getting home after the sun had already gone down. At this time, I knew that I had everything it took to be successful in a law practice, but moving to a new area and recently getting engaged to be married gave me pause. I was still journaling and goal setting, but concerns of where work would come from lingered. I would take one more job before finally stepping out into my own practice.

In law school, students were told that the law is like a jealous mistress requiring a long and constant courtship. Although I now realize that the statement is quite sexist, I've changed the word mistress to mister and found the analogy to be absolutely true. At times, it is a struggle to balance a personal life with a busy legal career. My close friends now say that I somehow manage to have more hours in the day than they do. I dare not tell them that the extra hours are sometimes due to lack of sleep, as I'm always searching for work- life balance.

My last job before becoming an entrepreneur was working for a South Florida law firm that ordered in breakfast, lunch and dinner because they never wanted the associates to leave the building solely for the purpose of food. The environment was somewhat reminiscent of the 1993 movie, "The Firm", minus Tom Cruise. It was the type of place where the money was great but everyone constantly complained of headaches, stress and anxiety. At that time, I regularly questioned my purpose in life. There was little opportunity to lead a more fulfilling life by incorporating community volunteerism activities that I loved. In the back of my mind I kept thinking, *"If I am going to work this hard, it needs to be for me"*. I wanted to create my own firm culture to include actually caring about people. Still, going out on my own did not appear to be an option. I had zero clients to take with me and I worked around the clock, including weekends. At this same time in 1998, I was planning my wedding and had just purchased a new home. How could I tell my then fiancé that I would be quitting my job and we would be living only on his income?

One month before our wedding, I went into the firm (a/k/a sweat shop) about 7:00 a.m. because I knew that I would be taking a longer lunch than usual that day. I had a scheduled wedding walk-through replete with a cake tasting. I worked until 11:00 a.m. before leaving the office to meet with my wedding planner. It was an exciting time, but also a stressful time trying to maintain billable hourly requirements and prepare for our special wedding day. I returned to the firm at approximately 12:30 p.m. and was greeted by the one person known within the firm as "the partner from hell." This partner wanted to know who I was with and why I was away from my desk for so long. As I looked at this partner in sheer disbelief, I knew that day would be my last day with that firm. The following morning, I turned in my keys and stood ready to become a law firm entrepreneur. I learned that disrespect was my trigger point and that if I were to continue practicing law at all, it would be only on my terms.

Initially after starting my own practice I worked from home. The attorneys at K&R referred me to a few personal injury cases and I got other work referrals from South Florida attorneys. I would wake up in the morning and get fully dressed by 6:15 a.m. as though I was leaving my home. There were exactly twenty-four steps from my bedroom to my home office. I gave my few clients intense attention. For the first time, I was determined to invest in myself, just as I had invested in all of the places where I had worked as an attorney. Additionally, I began to volunteer doing things that I loved to do. One of my most memorable local community experiences was planning a successful 5K run for the American Diabetes Association. We raised thousands of dollars and our efforts resulted in hundreds of runners coming out in support of the event. Those were things that I was not able to do prior.

Within a few months, I moved into a downtown office building directly across the street from the Broward County Courthouse. The building was owned by a former judge who took an instant liking to me and created space within his office that did not previously exist. In the first year of my private practice, I handled cases that I did not always want to handle. As time went on, and after investing 100% of my rainy-day funds into hiring my first associate, the business started to grow. The decision to chart my own professional course has worked for more than twenty years now. Upon reflection, one cannot underestimate being prepared. Whatever a person does to chart their own course should involve believing in your own talents and abilities, doing your best to treat others well, and knowing that you've put in the requisite time to understand your strengths and weaknesses and obtain some experience. Trying to maintain a culture of excellence, while also paying it forward, is a winning formula.

Here are a few things I've learned through trial and error:

1. **Keeping a positive attitude** and expressing frequent gratitude is important. My nature is to frequently say, *"Thank you"* to the people who work with me. I often say things like *"I really appreciate...."* This constant reassurance also lets people know, with certainty, that they are appreciated. These same people will want to produce their best work.

2. **Recruit the best talent that you can find.** Invest in the best talent that your budget will allow. Competent people will save you time and money. Word of mouth is great when it comes to recruiting talent, but utilize a formal

application or procurement process if informal networks fail to yield acceptable applicants.

3. **Strive to achieve longevity of your staff.** Staff longevity generally equals business stability. Keeping competent staff and trying to limit turnover is important. I've worked with some attorneys and staff for more than a decade. This type of stability has proven invaluable. Less disruption equals higher profits and peace of mind.

4. **Don't be afraid to grow**. You will need people who can help you cross the finish line when you run out of gas. This is critical to the sustainability and growth of your business. As a team, my law firm accomplishes a great deal each day. We operate like a well-oiled machine. When I first started my own law firm in the late 90's, for many years, I was afraid to grow beyond two or three attorneys. I had an unwarranted fear that with more people, there would be more headaches. I discovered, however, that the opposite is true. Growth has allowed my firm to fully service clients and has freed me up to be laser focused when those times become necessary.

5. **Learn all you can about your business before starting your business.** When I started my law practice in the late 90s, there were few books on the topic of starting a law practice. There were no support groups or blogs that I could find on the Internet. Now, there are so many resources, such as podcasts, internet videos and seminars available at the touch of a finger. If there is a will to be a successful entrepreneur, convenient information will be available to assist you.

6. **Support from family and friends is helpful.** I did not know how my then fiancé would react when I quit my job

a month before our wedding. He was exceptionally supportive. His faith in me gave me even more confidence in myself that success was not just a possibility, it was inevitable. Find support systems and people who will assist you in strategizing for success.

7. **Reducing overhead will help your bottom line.** I was fortunate to find office space that was below the market rate but still within the well-traveled area of the main Broward County Courthouse. For years, I enjoyed all of the benefits of being close to the courthouse, but paid a minimal amount of rent. One Sunday in 2003, after leaving church, I noticed a building that had a for sale sign hanging from the roof. Months later, I would be an owner of an office building while also paying less to own than most lawyers paid to rent in the downtown area of Fort Lauderdale. On nice days, I can walk to the state and federal courthouses. My office is also blocks away from a local train station with stops in Miami-Dade and Palm Beach counties. My office overhead is low and I am able to charge clients a fair price for my work without worrying about building in excessive overhead.

8. **You are only as good as your last win.** In running a business, it is important to know that you are only as good as your last win. Business owners must be committed to delivering excellence each and every day. Like it or not, in order for Black attorneys to run profitable law firms, you have to be three times better than others. Just being good will not be good enough. Strive for excellence each day.

9. **If you give yourself to the community, the community will give back to you.** I am one of the Founders of the Women of Color Empowerment Institute, Inc., a

501(c)(3), national organization with a mission to enhance and expand leadership by women of color. We hold a variety of programs, including, but not limited to professional mentorship programs and other initiatives focused on building and developing leadership skills. I love this organization with all of my being, and it keeps me quite busy. We have a weekly television show, a magazine, an office location, and we produce frequent events throughout the year. Additionally, I serve on local boards, such as the Fort Lauderdale Chamber of Commerce, Habitat for Humanity and lead committees for my local chapter of Delta Sigma Theta Sorority, Inc. and my local Links, Inc. Chapter. Community involvement is important to me. I prefer to work with others who care about and work in the community too. For lawyers looking to own their own firm, bar associations can be a good referral source for attorney entrepreneurs. I spent many years as a bar association junkie working with both local and national bar associations.

10. **Look for multiple streams of income.** I've always had an interest in ensuring that I had multiple sources of income. Having more disposable income has provided the flexibility to invest in researched opportunities that make financial sense. I'm constantly tinkering around with different business ideas. Not everything works out, but most do. One such business investment was in an office building located adjacent to my law office that is used by professionals, small businesses and traveling executives who want to maintain a convenient, attractive, Broward County office at a fraction of what it would cost to rent traditional office space. The concept of "Avenue Executive" was birthed when colleagues from out of town would occasionally take over my law firm conference room to prepare for their South Florida trials. Now, the

Avenue Executive space serves as office space, meeting space and as a rental facility for small events, such as baby showers and even wakes.

As I close, my advice to those thinking about starting a business is to jot down your goals and follow some of the tips above. I am a firm believer that with a proper foundation, the universe will make a way for anyone who aspires to do good.

About the Author
Dr. Nikki W. Hyppolite, RPh.

Dr. Nikki Wallace Hyppolite is a native Floridian, born of the Yamasee Tribal Nation. An overjoyed mother of two, influencer, and aspiring entrepreneur, she is determined to leave behind a legacy of self-awareness, prosperous entrepreneurs and spiritual guidance to impact the growth of health and wellness in excellence. Dr. Nikki graduated from Miami Norland Senior High School in 1992. She then moved on to higher education as a matriculating college student attending Florida A&M University located in Tallahassee, FL. She received her Doctorate of Pharmacy Degree in April of 2000.

Dr. Nikki has been an entrepreneur in the pharmaceutical industry for over twenty years, specializing in providing innovative healthcare through a variety of life enhancement programs that focus on health & wellness education, nutrition, fitness and individualized care. She has experience in pharmaceutical compounding; community retail pharmacy, hospital pharmacy and consulting for independent community pharmacy startups. Dr. Hyppolite currently provides customized health & wellness services and consulting services to fulfill private product design and development for clients.

She was chosen as one of the top Black-owned Businesses featured in Legacy Miami and Legacy South Florida Magazine in 2012. She was also recognized as one of the top twenty-five most prominent Black business Women in South Florida featured in Network Miami Magazine. She was recognized in *The Miami Times* and *The Miami Herald* for hosting Health Fairs and Educational Seminars at various churches and schools in the communities of Dade and Broward counties and she continues to give back to the community.

Chapter 12
Keep Going… Keep Growing!

Dr. Nikki Wallace Hyppolite, RPh
Compounding Pharmacist & Product Formulator

T here will always be a shift that will send you on the path that has been preordained for you when you are not doing what you are called to do. When it's in your DNA to be your own boss, you will not be content working for someone else for long. Being an entrepreneur is in my bloodline. In college, I chose the path to endure the six-year PharmD pharmacy program and graduated from FAMU with a Doctorate Degree of Pharmacy in the year of 2000. I interned with Walgreens and started with the company as a staff pharmacist, immediately passing the state board exam for the first time. I took the retail path because I felt that retail was the avenue in pharmacy that would enable me to connect with my purpose and work hands-on within the community. I only worked as a staff pharmacist for one year after graduating. The many jobs I had included Walgreens as an overnight pharmacist; a staff pharmacist at a hospital; I worked through an agency where I did seven days on and seven days off; and I worked for two independent pharmacies. I bounced around because I was looking for that feeling of fulfillment, but I just could not find it. I was doing the same things day after day with no autonomy to be creative, provide alternative health care options, or do other things for patients. I felt like a robot.

However, working for six-figures at each of those independent pharmacies, prepared me for what was coming in my future because I was able to observe the business side of running a pharmacy. That gave me the knowledge I needed when the time came for me to branch out on my own. In college, I learned how to work for someone else. I was not taught about the business or entrepreneurial side of pharmacy. I learned the business side on my own. Being able to learn the business gave me the insight and confidence I needed to step out on faith to open my own pharmacy.

PREPARING TO STEP OUT ON FAITH

While working for someone else, the thought of me operating my own pharmacy began to consume me on a daily basis. Although I was treated well, I was not content and could no longer continue having that feeling, so the day came when I finally made the decision to walk away and pursue my own dream. Prior to stepping out, I had prayed and asked God for guidance. I then put my vision in writing, starting with the name of the pharmacy. I called it 'Royalty' since I am a child of the royal priesthood. The complete name was 'Royalty Drugs & Pharmaceutical Care'. The research that I had conducted stated that one should set up an independent pharmacy in high income, affluent areas, but I wanted to work in an area that had the greatest need in order to be able to give back to the community. I then wrote down everything that needed to be done in order to put me in a position to have my own drug store. During this time, I consulted with a friend, an older woman, who had also been a mentor to me. We had worked together at the community health center as staff pharmacists during the time of my seven days off with Walgreens. We bonded and remained friends. She took me under her wings while we worked together. She had been in the pharmacy industry for many years, and at one time in her life, she had owned her own pharmacy as well, so she was able to give me lots of support, advice and guidance. She added fuel to the fire that was within me to start my own pharmacy business.

The day that I decided to resign from my job in order to branch out on my own and become a pharmacy owner, I did not know how my then-husband would respond to the news. At first, after listening to me tell him that I had quit my job, he gave me a blank stare, but I shared with him the plan that I had written down and I mapped out the specifics of the potential business with him. We discussed the startup cost as well as the potential ongoing costs. We talked about the potential target markets, the amounts that we would bill patients and I shared the name with him. After hearing the plan and discussing everything with him, he embraced the idea and told me that if the pharmacies I had worked for were able to pay me over six-figures a year, then obviously, there is money to be made in the industry and we can do it too. After delineating everything, he felt good about it. He saw that I had given it much thought and he understood that we had to take chances, but he was all in. He already was not happy where he was working, so he decided to leave his job, support the pharmacy, and became my business partner.

LAYING THE FOUNDATION

I filled out a community retail pharmacy application with the state of Florida and received my retail pharmacy license to operate as an independent pharmacy. Once I was approved, I received my pharmacy site number, which enabled me to open up accounts to get medications. Owning an independent pharmacy is like owning any other small business. Although the ultimate goal is to improve the lives of others, the overall business purpose is to make a profit. If the business doesn't profit, patients don't profit. I calculated the approximate amount of money that would be needed considering rent, the acquisition of products, designing the store, purchasing the pharmacy software program, staff salaries, licenses, knowledge or education that was needed, plus operating expenses for the months before the business started making a profit. I also knew that opening a pharmacy would require a significant financial risk, but we had a nice savings that was used to get started and I also got a few small business loans, which enabled us to set up the pharmacy. I calculated that our largest expense was going to be maintaining the prescription medication supply, realizing that we must always have enough on hand to meet monthly demand while ensuring that no medicine expired before it was dispensed. I developed a carefully thought-out operating budget.

A big advantage that I had was the fact that I was not only a pharmacy owner, but I was also *the* pharmacist-in-charge in my store. That was rare. There were many pharmacy owners at the time, but they were not actual pharmacists. I also had already established relationships with pharmacy representatives, so I was able to get the inventory that I needed for my store. When we first started off, it was myself, my then-husband, and two technicians who assisted me. My then-husband was the outreach liaison providing public relations opportunities for the business to flourish. He would go out into the community and develop relationships with staff members of a variety of doctors' offices and would also deliver medication to the patients, since we offered home-delivery service as well. The technicians did the patient intake process, made sure that the medications on the shelves were current and maintained daily tasks such as temperature checks to make sure our establishment was operating in excellence. After the pharmacy was set up, the state came in to do their inspections. In doing so, they inspected how the pharmacy was set-up; they made sure that we had certain protocols in place, such as the proper sinks, shelving, countertops and computers for an easy and productive workflow. They reviewed our policy procedural manuals, pharmacy protocols, how medication was refrigerated, reports that needed to be maintained, evidence of annual in-service with the pharmacy technicians, and they looked for evidence that the pharmacy technicians were licensed. The pharmacy inspector checked to make sure that we were complying with rules and regulations, as well as specifications within pharmacy laws and statues of the State of Florida. The business would not pass state inspection nor DEA requirements unless the entire pharmacy was built to specifications. With my background and experience working for so many different companies, I knew exactly what needed to be done and did it.

ROYALTY DRUGS AND PHARMACEUTICAL CARE

I did not want the pharmacy to have a drug store feel. I wanted it to be warm and inviting, so I was strategic with how I set up the inside of the store. I envisioned what the store would look like from the viewpoint of the patient walking through the doors for the first time. No matter how many times they came in, we wanted to impress them with our products and services. It was an inviting setting. We were not behind a plexiglass, but we set up our counter tops in compliance with the state and in comfort for the patients when meeting their prescription needs and personal expectations. I understood that those small things were the things that would get us talked about in the community. It took almost a month to get connected to insurance companies and third-party payors before we actually went live. What I got from the bank, coupled with what we had in savings allowed us to stay afloat before business started coming in. In the year 2001, we were set up and ready to go! We operated as a full-service Community Retail Pharmacy with convenient home or office delivery on the move. We had a storefront filled with food and convenient day to day needs just like any drug store chain set up today. The pharmacy department was positioned towards the back of the store.

Since I had been a pharmacy manager at a community health medical building in a low-income area, I was already familiar with the community and I knew that there was a great need there, so I opened my first pharmacy in that area. After opening, we had health fairs, contracts with community health centers and were able to provide

> *"I did not want the pharmacy to have a drug store feel. I wanted it to be warm and inviting, so I was strategic with how I set up the inside of the store."*

135

alternative healthcare to the patients, which was something I was not able to do while working for someone else. We provided a holistic approach that addressed the mind, body and spirit. I wanted to offer patients certain things that they did not get at traditional pharmacies, such as the time they needed for us to explain their medications, care regarding their concerns, current education, compassion, consistency, honor and respect, straightforward information, and ultimately going the extra mile for each patient. To ensure that our goals were accomplished, we would communicate with our patients by asking open-ended questions, such as if they knew why they were taking that medication and if they understood their conditions. It is all about the service that we provided that made the difference. The pharmacy was very successful and made an impact in the community. We ended up staying there for seven years until the owner sold the building and decided to turn it into apartments.

We moved the business to an area called Miami Gardens, which was about ten miles north of where we had been. The community was a bit different, but we were able to make our presence known there as well. We also did community health fairs and my then-husband was able to go out into the community and bring in more business. Even though we moved further away from our existing patients, they decided to stay with us and took advantage of our delivery service and still visited us from time to time.

COMPOUNDING

While in Miami-Gardens, I expanded the pharmacy brand to include compounding, which is putting two or more ingredients together to make a final product. My reason for taking courses in compounding was to put myself in a position to expand the business to be able to do more for our patients and clients. Many people think that pharmacists only count pills and fill prescriptions. It is more intricate than that. We take chemistry and biology courses; and those courses provide a better foundation for learning pathophysiology and pharmacology, which are two critical pillars of pharmacy education. Additionally, medicinal chemistry plays a vital role in providing critical thinking and evidence-based problem-solving skills to pharmacy students, enabling us to make optimal patient-specific therapeutic decisions. Pharmacists know more about medications than the doctors do because we know how the drugs are broken down and what they do to every organ in the body from the time a patient puts them in their mouth until the time they are excreted. We literally have the lives of patients in our hands. For this reason, they have now included pharmacists on the medical teams that make rounds in the hospitals because they realize that pharmacists are an important piece to the puzzle for solving problematic health conditions.

Compounding gave me an opportunity to be more patient specific at the pharmacy. I made products for patients based on their individual conditions and body types. For example, when I had patients who were on Polypharmacy, meaning they were on multiple medications, generally three or more a day to treat poor health conditions and were not compliant in taking all of them, compounding allowed me to turn some of the medications into a cream or a liquid to make it easier for them to be compliant in taking care of themselves. The skin absorbs ingredients as if you were to take them by mouth. Making a difference in the lives of people through compounding has given me a great sense of fulfillment.

The pharmacy began doing so well that big retailers would call to ask if I was interested in selling. For some reason, they knew that we had a large patient base. They also knew the quality of service that we provided because it was well known in the community, so for some reason, we would always get calls to sell. Our business was doing well, but unfortunately, things started changing…

POLICY AND LEGISLATIVE CHANGES

In the past, patients had been able to get their prescriptions filled wherever they wanted to, but when things started changing, they had to go where their insurance company told them to go. They had no choice. If they went outside of their network, then they would have to pay. Many of our patients did not have money to pay copays, nonetheless to pay out of network to get their prescription filled with us. That is how we began to lose many of our customers and ultimately started losing lots of money. Every year, the National Community Pharmacists Association (NCPA) releases the NCPA Digest. This report compiles data from independent pharmacies across the nation. The Digest shows that the average independent pharmacy profit margin used to be steady and reliable. However, that changed. In 2009, gross profits steadily declined. *"Most of the decrease came over the past four years, caused by below-cost reimbursement and unpredictable DIR fees in Medicare Part D,"* according to the Digest.

When the industry shifts and the laws change, it affects many businesses, usually for the worst. Oftentimes, we don't even see it coming. As business owners, we get accustomed to operating on what we have coming in and going out, but when we don't get as much coming in anymore, adjustments must be made. When Medicare part D was implemented, it made a big shift in the elderly population to where they had to pay for their own medicine. Many times, they could not afford it, so we would help them by providing medication at no cost. That was no money coming in, but I was still helping the community, which has always been my focus. At some point, the legislative changes affected all of my employees and I got to the point to where I did not want to continue fighting that fight with policy changes that significantly affected the pharmacy. During that time, I was also blindsided in my marriage and was going through a divorce. My then-husband had been my business partner and I could not wear both hats, the PR hat and the Pharmacy Manager hat. I needed to be in a good headspace for my two children because they required a lot of my time that I was not willing to compromise for anything or anyone. My children were and will always be my number one priority. Policy changes happening in the pharmaceutical industry coupled with my marital problems, forced me to make the decision to sell the business. I sold my pharmacy to a friend who had a pharmacy in an adjacent county. After I sold the pharmacy and got divorced, I purchased a pediatric office because I wanted to have passive income without being present at the business every day. I chose this option to bring together medical and pharmaceutical services to meet the needs of newborns, kids, teens, young adults and parents. I wanted to provide convenience for any patient in need of medications that needed to start therapy ASAP such as antibiotics, anti-inflammatories, antipyretics, etc. I employed a Pediatrician to care for the patients and I served as the in-house Pharmacist. I had that for three years and then sold that business also. I realized that I needed to marry my profession with my passion. I am a problem solver and addressing health concerns with customized patient care is my true calling and gift. Therefore, formulating and product production is where I do my greatest good to the world.

APE JEWEL INNOVATIONS, INC

As of this writing (July, 2021), I am the President/CEO of Ape Jewel Innovations, Inc. I consult, formulate and produce product(s) for individuals who want private labeled products to sell on the market. I give consultations to find out what they specifically want their products to do, how they want their products to look, smell, feel and most importantly, how they want their clients to feel once they purchase the products. They tell me what their vision is and what their end goals are for their products. Once I acquire all of that information, I develop formulas for their products throughout the research and development stage. When I get the ingredients, I inform them on what each ingredient does. For example, I have a client who has a massage therapy business who specializes in manual therapy. His client base consists of professional athletes, high school athletes and other athletic individuals. He wanted a product that improved flexibility, increased blood flow, decreased inflammation and dissolves cramps instantly upon application. I have another client for whom I formulate a total skin-care line. I make pills, capsules, lotions, etc. These products are non-prescription products used with natural ingredients that do the same things that most chemical ingredients do, but I am more on the natural, alternative side. I have been compounding since 2007 and many clients come to me through word of mouth. I love what I am now doing, and I do not regret opening two pharmacies because it was rewarding and made a significant impact on the surrounding communities.

As I look back, I realize that the nine jobs that I had prior to opening my own pharmacy prepared me to operate my own. I was able to see how the pharmaceutical industry operated in various entities and it helped me significantly when operating my own pharmacy. Had I not stepped out on faith to do something that was in my belly, I would still be unfulfilled and miserable to this day. I am no longer a pharmacy owner, but I am still an entrepreneur. I have succeeded in every business venture that I have had and I love what I do. Just because one business does not work out, that does not mean that you stop pursuing entrepreneurship. The experience that did not work out could have been designed only for learning so that when your true calling is ready for you to take hold of it, you will be qualified, experienced and ready.

ADVICE TO ASPIRING ENTREPRENEURS

If you have a feeling on the inside of you that will not allow you to be content with what you are currently doing because you have a strong desire to branch out on your own, then prepare to take that leap of faith. My advice is to pray about it first. Then, put your vision in writing. Activate what you put in writing and seek wise counsel from people who are already in the field. Develop relationships with the right people who are willing to help you. Be active in your field. Know what is happening in your industry. Get your business name and register with your state. Find the right bank to open your account. If you want to open an actual brick and mortar, find the right location. Keep praying as you continue to progress and be willing to inspire others. Put yourself in position to succeed. If you don't have the guts, you won't get the glory!

About the Author
Lisa Ivory

 Lisa Ivory was born and raised in Miami, Florida and continues to reside in South Florida. She is the CEO of, The Ivory Group, a certified minority and woman-owned business. As CEO of The Ivory Group, Lisa is responsible for business development, securing partnerships, contract management, and overseeing day-to-day operations.

She began her career working for the State of Florida in Tallahassee overseeing testing and training programs statewide before transitioning to Broward County Public Schools (the 6th largest school district in the US) as former Assessment & Accountability Manager. Lisa was also a consultant for Educational Testing Service, and the State Account Manager for Pearson. She is highly regarded in her field.

Lisa is a former board member of the Florida Juvenile Justice Foundation and serves as an advisor to JackieTrust, an organization founded to teach and empower children of color to build a stock and investment portfolio before they reach adulthood. She is a member of the International Mastermind Association and is co-author of 'No Glory without a Story' (Edition 1).

She received her undergraduate degree in Communications from Fort Valley State College and a Masters Degree of Public Policy from Florida A&M University.

Lisa is a proud member of the South Broward Alumnae Chapter of Delta Sigma Theta, Sorority, Inc., and The Greater Fort Lauderdale Chapter of Jack & Jill of America, Inc. These organizations all have a direct impact and emphasis on educating and empowering youth. Lisa is married to Melvin, and they have two sons Landon and Dylan.

Chapter 13
Leaving the Corporate World to Start a Family Business

Lisa Ivory

CEO, The Ivory Group

My husband and I own and operate an electrical contracting company. We consider ourselves a baby company, but we are growing and progressing fast. I am the CEO of 'The Ivory Group' and my husband is the President. It was in 2019 when we decided to really put our time, energy and effort into building our family business. We were already incorporated as an LLC and had been filing business taxes for the past five years. When we started doing business on the scale that we are doing now, we were able to show that we had technically been in business for at least five years.

I worked in educational sales for over ten years, which is a very lucrative, yet fickle industry. I was laid off at the end of 2018, which was about the third time in my sales career. After the last layoff, I told my husband that I did not desire to go back to work, although I was getting many calls from other companies and recruiters. I could have gotten another job easily, but I was tired of the required travel in that industry and I wanted to be home with my children more. I told my husband that if he was OK with me not going back to work, I would stay home and help him build his business while also being home more with our children. Working full time for his business was something my husband had always wanted, and I wanted to make sure that it was done right. When 2019 rolled around, I used my time towards laying the foundation and building his business up. I took a few certification courses, created our business website and logo, and I reached out to general contractors who I knew were successful in the construction industry. I sought advice and counsel from them, which proved to be extremely valuable. I took in all that I could and learned as much as I could in getting started. I had no idea what God had in store for us for us.

GETTING INTO POSITION

My husband previously worked for a company that received a lucrative government contract. The agency liked him so much that when a new company received the contract, they asked the new company to hire him. Because of his skills, he was encouraged to get his master license so that he could pursue contracts. In fact, the one that he was working on, would be up for renewal in a few years. My husband shared with me that he wanted to be in a position to pursue that particular government contract when it came back around, so that became our main goal. I was determined to get our business off the ground, so I went back to school and became certified as a project manager so that I would be able to oversee the planning and construction of projects from beginning to end. I also became certified in Lean Six Sigma, which is a method that provides businesses with the tools they need to improve business processes and cut waste. I also attended a federal Small Business Administration (SBA) workshop to learn about different programs available to assist small minority-owned businesses. The federal government is the largest purchaser in the world, spending billions of dollars annually on contracts for materials, goods and services.

During this time, my husband was studying to take the master certification exam. He went to Orlando for one week to take a prep class that prepared him for the exam. We were told by a few contractors that he would not pass the first time, but not to be discouraged. However, he passed the exam his very first time taking it! Although he successfully passed the exam on his first attempt, he had to apply to the state board in order to receive his master electrician license. Initially the board denied his application, but it was a clear sign of being delayed, not denied! We put together a package that included pictures of work and experience as well as recommendation letters from those in the industry. The next time the board met, he went in person to state his case, and was granted his Master Electrician license. This put us in the position to pursue government contracts. I signed up to receive alerts of government agency contracts that were released, and we began attending workshops on the process to become a certified minority-owned business. To qualify for the contract we wanted to pursue, we had to be a certified vendor with a particular brand. We pursued a partnership with the distributor and became a certified distributor. We were putting things in position in 2019 to be able to take off in 2020.

The government contract that my husband wanted to pursue came up in 2020, but for some reason, I did not get the notice. When I learned the RFP was out, we had less than a week to put together our bid. I had also missed the informational meeting. However, I had already done my research on the past contracts awarded by this agency on similar bids. This was my first time ever submitting a bid for a contract with a governmental agency, so I looked up who received the previous contracts, what their package entailed and what they offered. I studied the highest bidder and the lowest. This process came with lots of sleepless nights and stress. There were mandatory requirements of the contract that we did not meet, and after relentless efforts we kept running into roadblocks. My husband would say, *"Don't stress over it. We will just go after it next time."* My response, however was, *"No we are going to pray that God creates a path to meet this requirement."* ...AND HE DID! All proposals were due on a specific day at 2:00p.m. Around noon on the day it was due, a miracle happened, and we received the final requirement needed to submit our proposal! The final package was submitted at 1:58 p.m.

AN ANSWERED PRAYER

While waiting on the outcome of the proposal, we received a call from one of the general contractors that I previously sought advice from. They wanted to know if we had a crew available to assist on a major project. We met with their company, reviewed the terms, visited the site, reviewed the blueprints, and assembled a team. At that time, my husband was still working full-time with another company. We prayed about the decision, stepped out on faith and he resigned from his full-time job. We both began working full-time for our business, The Ivory Group. Our full-time jobs entailed my husband working 10-12 hours in the field, overseeing projects, and supervising employees. I managed our contract deliverables, invoicing, payroll, ordering supplies and materials and proposal development. That general contractor has been a blessing to the Ivory Group. They are leaders in the industry and have provided a multitude of opportunities to work on large contracts with a variety of agencies.

While we awaited the outcome of our very first government proposal, I received a few phone calls from a young lady in the procurement department requesting clarification on different aspects of our proposal. I was not sure if this was customary and if they were calling everyone for clarification of certain things. I finally asked them when the results would be released. I was told that the information would be on the website shortly, and when I looked, I saw that we were the recommended company for a multi-year, million-dollar contract! That moment was amazing! ...and it felt surreal! We were told by a few vendors that we were incredibly lucky to get the contract because they had assisted several seasoned companies with their proposals. Getting that contract was an amazing accomplishment, but we needed to really get in position to be able to deliver and we needed funds to get started. When opportunity knocks, you must be prepared to answer. We were not successful in securing business loans as we did not have a record of this magnitude of business so we pulled financial resources from every pocket we could. This included personal savings, retirement plans, insurance claims, stocks, bonds, etc. My husband assembled a team who would be dedicated to fulfilling the obligations of this contract.

GROWING PAINS

There are some frustrating days and growing pains, but we work through them and find lessons in each one. There were times when we would put a team together to work around the clock because we had tight deadlines. When those days happen, we must pay our employees overtime, but there were times that the money was not there because it was not coming in quick enough. Government contracts can take anywhere from 60-90 days to pay. However, as a small business, you have to figure out how to keep your employees paid while you are waiting to get paid. Employees are used to getting paid weekly, so we had to do what we could to make sure that the funds to pay them are there. When payday arrives employees do not want to hear any excuses as to why they cannot get paid. They too have families and bills to pay. There was a time when I picked up a check just in time to make payroll for the week. However, the bank had a seven-day hold policy and would not make any exceptions. I stood outside of the bank crying because I never wanted to be in a position where we couldn't pay our team. By the grace of God, my mother came through for us and the employees got paid on time. It is the behind-the-scenes situations like that that those looking in from the outside do not know about. We're learning and growing with each passing day on how to effectively manage the business and cash flow, which is essential. Due to human error, there were times that we had to stop and redo work that we had already completed. When this happens, we must go back and pay employees to make the necessary corrections. This can be extremely frustrating, but we must stand by our work and ensure that all completed projects meet contractual obligations and most of all exceeds client expectations.

A GLIMPSE INTO THE FUTURE

When I was in grad school, I worked for a temp agency as a receptionist at an electrical office. The calls for servicing would come to me. I remember that there was a particular company that had contracts with the different supermarkets, hotels, and schools. When they would get calls, I would route the calls and send people out. As I look back now, I see that as a foreshadowing of things to come. In our first year, we have been blessed with a contract with a governmental agency, projects at public schools, and local colleges. Unfortunately, we turn down quite a few projects because we do not have the capacity to take everything that is coming our way. We want to expand, but not too fast to where we cannot sustain. My husband works extremely hard going from jobsite to jobsite every day and he will not ask anyone to do anything that he would not do himself. It is a blessing to see him finally enjoying the fruit of his labor. Although we have had to turn down some projects, in this business, you must keep projects in the pipeline. For example, although you may be awarded a project today, the work may not begin for another year or two. Therefore, if we don't keep a steady flow of projects in the pipeline, when the current projects are complete, there will be no projects to keep funding coming in and staff employed. I am constantly pursing new business opportunities while my husband runs the day to day operations in in the field.

WORKING WITH YOUR SPOUSE

There are times when working with my husband can be frustrating. I must remind him that I am the CEO of The Ivory Group. As such, I am the one who signs the checks. I also must remind him that we are a minority and woman-owned business by the state and the county, and to be a minority *and* woman-owned business, a WOMAN has to own at least 51% of the company. I am NOT your secretary! …but at the end of the day, we are partners and I have no intentions of returning to the corporate world. I am grateful to have had the opportunity to set the foundation for our family business. Taking that leap of faith to go after contracts has paid off for us. I do not regret not going back to work and I am proud of the accomplishments that we have made thus far. The money we make goes back into our business, not into someone else's business. Since taking off in 2020, our business has prospered, but every day in this business is busy. May, 2021 marks one year since the business took off. At this juncture, I do not see myself going to work for anyone else anymore. I work for The Ivory Group, this *is* my full-time job.

ADVICE TO ASPIRING ENTREPRENEURS

If you follow your dreams, you will be surprised at what you can accomplish. If you have a desire to start your own business and you are not content working for an organization or a company, then pray about it first. Don't just up and quit your job with no plan for how you will get started. Map out a plan consisting of your vision, then develop goals for your business. Find a good mentor in the business - someone that you look up to, who will guide you right and who will not mind imparting knowledge into you. Learn as much as you can about your industry and do research. Choose a name for your business, get registered with the state, develop your website, get your company logo and research what needs to be done to get started. Entrepreneurship can be very rewarding - especially when it comes to creating generational wealth. We desire to leave a legacy for our children and their children. I now stress entrepreneurship with my children; and my husband and I are planting the seeds in them now. Do not ever underestimate what you are able to do when you put your mind, your thoughts, your talents and energy into pursuing your goals.

> *"Taking that leap of faith to go after contracts has paid off for us. I do not regret not going back to work and I am proud of the accomplishments that we have made thus far."*

About the Author
Michelle Swaby-Smith

 Michelle Swaby-Smith has owned and operated a successful Florida based firm that specializes in product and event promotions, event planning, medical meeting management, business meeting management, show management, show production, street team promotions, as well as artist/talent management. She has served the Florida market for over 23 years and has gained a reputation of excellence. Ms. Swaby-Smith has also been involved in the entertainment industry for many years and has been very successful in establishing lasting relationships with key players in all facets of the industry. These relationships have been forged through her work in management at Carnival Cruise Lines, as Chief Promotional and Production Coordinator for the Cancun Jazz Festival (3 years), PGPP Enterprises, Inc., Big Blue & You, Inc., and Vice President of a Martial Arts Academy. She has been involved with many successful events in the South Florida and Caribbean areas such as, Art by the Sea, Umoja Festival, Miami Carnival, American Black Film Festival, Spirit Airlines Corporate Meetings, Jazz in the Gardens, and Event Producer for Women's Impact Conference & Luncheon, just to name a few.

Michelle currently consults as the Special Events Liaison at the Historic Virginia Key Beach Park, helps to run Next Level Martial Arts Academy with her husband, manages the career of her super star daughter, Danni Washington, and is co-founder of the non-profit Big Blue & You, Inc. The Big Blue & You is a 501(c)(3) Non-Profit organization that focuses on educating, inspiring and empowering youth through arts, science and media. The organization was started in 2008 and is doing many initiatives in the Florida and the Caribbean markets to involve young people in the communities. Michelle has been a volunteer with Big Brother Big Sister of Broward and was recognized as 'Big Sister of the Year' in 2009.

Chapter 14
Transitioning from Employee to Employer

Michelle Swaby-Smith
President/CEO, P.G.P.P. Enterprises, Inc.

M ichelle Swaby-Smith was how I told my husband I would have to incorporate his last name when we got married. I explained that the name Michelle Swaby was a "*Brand*" in South Florida and there was no way that I could just be "Michelle Smith". I'm a proud Jamaican-born woman who made the decision many years ago to come to the United States with my family, make South Florida our home and become a U.S. citizen. My Caribbean roots are strong and will always be the foundation of all that I am. I have been blessed to have always had an entrepreneurial spirit and definitely used that fire to run my businesses for over 23 years now. Currently, there are four companies that I own, co-own, and manage. The first is my Event and Meeting Management Firm - P.G.P.P. Enterprises, Inc. (**P**roduct **G**rowth **P**romotions & **P**roductions), then there's the no
n-profit that my daughter and I started in 2008 called Big Blue & You, Inc. - Ocean & Environmental Conservation Education/Inspiration for Youth. Third, there is Big Blue Enterprises, LLC, which is a for profit company established for my daughter, Danni Washington's career as a TV Host, Producer, Marine Biologist, and Science Communicator. Lastly, my husband and I operate a martial arts

academy called 'Next Level Martial Arts Academy'. We do not have employees at any of the companies, but I have hired hundreds of independent contractors over the years and my philosophy has always been that we are all a part of a "Team". Operating my businesses has been extremely rewarding, not just for me, but for the many people who have joined forces with us and became part of the companies.

IN THE BEGINNING

From the time I was a little girl, I have always been an organizer. When we had sleepovers with my cousins, I was the one who coordinated the "Fashion Shows" that we did, and my aunt used to always ask my mom, *"Why isn't Michelle in the Fashion Show?"* My mom's response was always the same: *"Because she's the Organizer."* As the years went by, my love and passion for animals took me on a path to study and become a Veterinary Technician. I worked in that field for many years at various animal hospitals in South Florida and even though the work was rewarding, I needed a change, so in 1985, I decided that I wanted to explore other career options. This quest led me to apply for a job at Carnival Cruise Lines (CCL) in the accounting department. What was so ironic about this position was that I had always hated math in school. However, I was hired by CCL to help coordinate the Accounts Receivable Department because they were just starting the company at that time and that department did not exist. Several years into my tenure at CCL, I was promoted to Accounts Receivable Supervisor/Manager and that was the position that I held at the time that I resigned in 1997, which was my 12th year at the company.

WHEN OPPORTUNITY KNOCKS

In 1997, I was presented with an opportunity through a friend in Chicago. He had landed a marketing deal with a major liquor distributor who was interested in doing some promotional concepts in the South Florida market. I had the experience because while I was working at the cruise lines all those years, I had also been coordinating parties, promotions, and events with a promoter friend who was well established in the entertainment industry. The experience taught me a lot and prepared me for this amazing opportunity that was offered to me. I don't know how I found the time or energy to do it all, but when you do what you love, it's not hard to make great things happen! Needless to say, I accepted the offer and started a promotional company. I was ecstatic at the idea of owning my own business!

The hardest thing about stepping out on your own after being in the corporate world for so long is taking that FIRST STEP. However, the actual process that is needed to establish your own business is really not difficult. The task list includes, but is not limited to the following:

1. Creating a name for your company
2. Creating a business plan (there are many samples of business plans online)
3. Registering your company with the IRS and obtaining your EIN number
4. Registering your company with the state in which you live and plan to do business. (In the state of Florida, it is SunBiz)
5. Set up your business bank accounts
6. Decide if you want a business partner. Hire independent contractors/staff/employees if applicable. (In my case, it was models/promo girls/guys, etc.)
7. Secure several clients by marketing your business
8. Create a website and social media presence on Instagram, Facebook and Twitter
9. Set goals and projections for at least three years ahead
10. Do research on the clients that you are targeting for business and always strive to exceed your clients' expectations.

After all of that was done, I was ready to start working on the project by October of 1997 - all while still working at Carnival Cruise Lines. Once the project was executed, I very quickly realized that I was making more money in three days of managing those promotions (at 3-4 hours each time) than I was making at CCL working five days a week for eight hours a day. I took a giant leap of faith and turned in my resignation to CCL in December of 1997. I even forfeited my year-end bonus because I was so ready to be free of the corporate world and ready to be a business owner! I learned so much from being at an amazing corporation for so many years and I still loved CCL and my "family" colleagues, but it was time to *"Transition from an Employee to Employer"*. ...and that's exactly what I did. I have never regretted that decision.

A FRESH START & NEW ADVENTURE

The first six years of running P.G.P.P. Enterprises, Inc. were exciting, prosperous, and very rewarding. I brought on a business associate after my first year in business when I realized that it was absolutely too much for one person to handle alone - especially one person who just transitioned from corporate to total entrepreneurship. My business associate was very good with finances and would make magic happen with the coordination of the deals that were sent our way. My main responsibility was to manage the operations and execution of the projects. It worked well for many years until we decided to part ways. The only advice I would give on going into business with friends is to make sure that the lines are definitively drawn in the company and everyone is clear on their positions, responsibilities and expectations. Unclear boundaries can ruin both friendships and business relationships if not clearly defined from the onset. Unfortunately, many relationships between "friends going into business together", have been

> *"I took a giant leap of faith and turned in my resignation…. I even forfeited my year-end bonus because I was so ready to be free of the corporate world and ready to be a business owner!"*

ruined because of unclear boundaries, poor communication, trust issues and unscrupulous behavior.

When I first started P.G.P.P. Enterprises, Inc., the first client that I acquired was interested in having my company manage promotions in the South Florida urban and Hispanic markets at first. However, within a year, that client added the entire state of Florida to our portfolio. That meant a lot of traveling for me. As my company went into each market in the state of Florida, we were responsible for hiring independent contractors (models), training them and executing the projects. Doing this meant meeting and interacting with many people. I realized early on that there is a certain skill-set that is needed to interact with so many varying personalities. One of the most important tools that I used in my company was to make sure that every person who signed on with us was called a "Team Member" and treated like a very important part of the company. It is important that everyone is on the same page for the success of a project and that everyone is given the feeling of inclusion. The "Team Member" concept versus "employee" or "worker" is one of the best practices that I believe every company should adopt. It breeds unity and camaraderie. Team members take initiative, seek out opportunities to contribute, and don't always need to wait to be given directives. Employees generally only focus and do the work that is assigned to them. As an entrepreneur, supervisor or manager, you cannot expect anyone to work at optimal levels, go over and beyond, or produce maximum performance when they are treated as an outsider, made to feel like just a worker, or unappreciated. There is so much value in the "Team" Concept.

As the years went by, my company's client base grew through word of mouth and industry connections. It is crucial to always maintain a high level of integrity, professionalism, decorum, patience, power, and honesty. The best advertisement is word of mouth and when the word gets out that you are an honest business professional who operates with integrity, it draws clients to you. A good business reputation cannot be overstated. In like manner, when you do not operate ethically, word gets out just the same and can negatively impact not only your business, but your reputation. The independent contractors that we hired tended to stay with our company for several years at a time because they were always treated with respect and inclusion. This made for a successful business in many ways. The financial part was wonderful, but it was the long-term relationships, business connections, and friendships that were the real wins. Those last forever!

GROWING PAINS, CHALLENGES & TRIUMPHS

If owning your own business was easy, then everyone would do it. It's not difficult, but it's just not for everyone. Entrepreneurs are wired differently than individuals who like the comfort of knowing that there is a steady income if they get up every day and go to a job - whether they like it or not. Most people who are in the nine to five workforce usually hate their jobs but would rather be an employee for the ease of mind and security of a paycheck. Owning your own business usually means that there are really no days off (unless you force yourself), long days of work, sleepless nights, lots of responsibilities, many demands that come from different directions, people constantly depending on you, and most of all, it is usually the only source of income for a person who decides to take this path. However, the rewards far outweigh the daunting negatives. When I first started my business, I made sure that I had enough funds available to sustain me for at least four months (six months is optimum). With that in place, it gave me the freedom to move without the pressures of the daily and monthly expenses in my life.

Once I made the decision to be my own boss, I knew that failure was not an option! When the growing pains came in the first year or so of the business, I had already built a roadmap for success and was prepared to do everything I could to break through any deterrents. That roadmap included forecasting one year ahead with the new client and also projecting that my company would definitely land more clients throughout the year. It also included putting a large percentage of revenue back into the company and getting rid of any unproductive team members who were not looking out for the best interest of the company. The most difficult part of my growing pains was that we would have to say *"no"* to certain companies due to their values not aligning with ours. When you are growing your business, the act of refusing clients and saying no to well-needed funds, is very difficult to do, but if you don't have a moral compass, your company could derail very quickly. Staying strong in your fundamental principles is paramount and will serve you well throughout your life in business and otherwise.

I have owned my own business for over 23 years as of this writing and although it has not always been easy, it's definitely been rewarding. The freedom that I have experienced is priceless! I must reiterate however, that not everyone is wired to be an entrepreneur. Not everyone is cut out to motivate themselves and make things happen everyday. Not everyone has the willpower to not be idle or unproductive when they are working from home. As an entrepreneur, you have no time to sit idly by and let hours go by without getting important tasks completed. You cannot waste time watching your favorite TV shows if there are crucial items on your To-Do list that need to be completed and you're on timelines. …but one thing is for sure, everyone **does** have the ability to push themselves beyond their comfort zones and do all they can to achieve their dreams. If you are willing to make the sacrifices, lose some sleep and forgo some pleasures at times, you can be a successful business owner; but you must be willing to put in the time, sweat and even tears at times. Keep in mind that being the best at anything that you do, including owning your own business, takes resilience, tenacity, focus, drive, fortitude, humility, faith, strength, and most of all, the belief that you can achieve what you set your mind to do.

ADVICE TO ASPIRING ENTREPRENEURS
Entrepreneurs of all ages and with various levels of experience face internal doubts when thinking about whether or not they have what it takes to run their own business. There is a lot of detail to think about and processes to put in place. If there is one trait that

entrepreneurs have in common, it's the ability to set goals. Start by identifying what your overall company purpose is, and develop smaller, achievable goals that serve as stepping stones to achieving that purpose. Those small goals will not only make your company's purpose more achievable and less intimidating, but will give you a good indication of where to actually begin. If you are thinking about taking a leap of faith and transitioning from employee to employer, I hope that my story has inspired you to make the move. Do your research and due diligence in the area that you wish to pursue. Apply your God-given skills, talent and intellect. Take good advice from experts and true friends. Then plan, plan, plan, pray and just go for it! Wishing you all abundant blessings!

About the Author

Akino & Jamila West

 Chef Akino has spent the last ten years of his career working his way up the culinary ladder by beginning as a line cook and student of the world of culinary arts. After excelling in vocational programming while in high school, Akino decided to make the progressive move by attending Johnson & Wales University in North Miami Beach, FL. After four years of dedication, Chef Akino graduated with his Bachelor's Degree in Food Service Management while working his way up to becoming an Executive Sous. His wife, Jamila attended The Culinary Institute of America in Hyde Park, New York after years of training while in high school. Jamila received a Bachelor of Science Degree in Hospitality Management from Johnson & Wales University. Jamila has spent years growing, learning, and advising within the hospitality industry internationally. They both have worked under some of the best chefs &hospitality groups of the current time. In 2013, Jamila was recognized as a Collaborate Business Magazine's "30 under 30" professional to be on the watch for. This power couple are the founders of The Copper Door B&B and Rosies Restaurant located in Overtown, Miami. They are known and recognized as having some of the best food in the Overtown area.

Chapter 15

Manifesting the Business Dream that God gave You

Akino & Jamila West

Hotel & Restaurant Business Owners

W hen there is a strong vision on the inside of you to start your own business, you will never be satisfied working for someone else. Rosie's, our pop-up restaurant in Overtown, Miami was birthed out of a need to find a way to sustain ourselves during the Covid 19 pandemic. The national pandemic had shut everything down, so many businesses all over the United States had come to an abrupt halt, but that is not where the story begins…

While attending Johnson and Wales University in 2015, I began working as a line cook at Michael's Genuine Food and Drinks. The chef/owner gave me the opportunity to experience what "local" truly means from the standpoint of patronizing businesses that are all local. My time there was unparalleled and was genuinely the start of my career. Day in and day out while working there, I could not help but think about the fact that I was helping to make someone else's dream successful. I continued learning, growing, and eventually landing a position at Noma, a Michelin star-rated restaurant in Copenhagen, Denmark. It would be the first time I had ever traveled outside of the country besides the Caribbean islands. After being in Denmark for eight months, I traveled for another four months. I was in Europe for about a year totaled and learned so much. The motivation to own something of my own grew stronger. At this time, I had been a dedicated culinarian for about thirteen years.

MERGING OUR GOALS

My girlfriend at the time, Jamila Ross, started working in the restaurant industry as a teenager and well into her 20s. She and I first met at Johnson & Wales and ended up reconnecting about three years later. We began dating and learned that we both were at a pivotal point in our lives where creating something sustainable was equally a goal for both of us. We were both working full-time jobs and would often chat about our individual aspirations and would discuss what a dream reality could look like. For her, it was to own a bed and breakfast. For me, it was to own a restaurant. After working many long nights and helping Jamila manage someone's Airbnb properties as a side hustle, we decided to take the first step of many as a business couple by investing in a home in Buena Vista West, a residential neighborhood in the heart of Miami, Florida. We furnished the home and began marketing it on Airbnb as a vacation rental property. The home was a 4-bedroom, 2-bathroom that was artsy and fun while homey and comfortable. The business was special to us both and did quite well, although it was not quite enough to feed our hunger for entrepreneurship.

After operating and owning the Airbnb for about a year and a half, I got the itch to finally begin investigating restaurant spaces. We began meeting with realtors and developers to explore opportunities. After sharing our only business at the time, the Airbnb concept, one of the developers we had been working with informed us that he owned a 22-room boutique hotel building in Overtown, Miami. The building was built in 1942 and had been vacant for about 20 years, although it had a rich history, opportunity for multiple restaurant/hospitality space and had a history of Black entrepreneurship. During our first tour of the building, my impression was that the space was clearly condemned, dilapidated and run down. However, Jamila was able to see the vision of what could be possible and how important the historical nature of the property would be to future generations. While my eyes opened wide at the shock of how decrepit the building was, her eyes lit up at the vision of what the space could become. With 22 guest rooms, 22 bathrooms, and a large lobby that was perfect to host breakfast, it was certainly worth investigating. I am originally from Riviera Beach, Florida, about two hours North of Miami and had no knowledge of the history of Overtown. During the process of leasing the building, I listened to neighbors, mentors, and people who were familiar with the history of Overtown. I learned of how important that particular area is to Miami's history and Black history in general. During the 1940's through the 1970's, Overtown was known as a cultural hub for the best food and music made by and made for African Americans, from the rich and famous to those finding their way.

TAKING A LEAP OF FAITH

Jamila and I ended up quitting our comfortable jobs, for a journey that would change our lives forever! We made the decision to invest our savings, blood, sweat and tears into this dream. We worked day and night to create a solid business plan, to pitch our story to the community and search for any additional funding we could. Start-up concepts are not generally something loan opportunities are interested in. We quickly realized that without business history or enough funding on our side, we would have to get creative to achieve our goal. After grueling negotiations, we decided to bring our landlords into the deal, and they agreed to furnish the space. This gave us the leverage and less financial risk to counter what we didn't have with what we did - the skills to create a great guest experience. Jamila and I virtually did everything. Between us, we were the receptionists, the marketing team, housekeepers, the

> *"Jamila and I ended up quitting our comfortable jobs, for a journey that would change our lives forever."*

bookkeepers, the chefs, and security. The budget was very tight, and we leaned on internship programming for a bit of help. As the business began to grow, so did our team.

THE COPPER DOOR B&B

The original hotel from 1942 was named, The Demetree Hotel by James "Jimmy Demetree" then Moon's Home by second-generation predecessor, Carl "Moon" Mullins. After almost four years in, we named the business 'The Copper Door B&B' - a genuine hospitality concept where Miami's African American history, art, and culinary expertise thrive through our guest experience. Jamila and I are ambassadors of our city by encouraging visitors within our 22-guestrooms to explore neighborhoods of culture and history of Miami. We create an intimate travel experience for our guests by recommending local hang outs and events. We host like-minded individuals in a communal, comfortable setting in order to have unique conversations and explore Miami through different perspectives.

We are so thankful that The Copper Door B&B has been progressively successful since opening on July 1, 2018. We honestly did not know what to expect. Initially we received a few bookings here and there, but when the positive reviews started flowing, so did more and more reservations. We had a great time interacting with guests and showing off a different Miami culture. Around 85% of the guests were there because they had booked Caribbean cruises. They would book a night with us the day prior to their cruise departure and book a night the following week before returning back home. We take great pride in making genuine connections with our guests and it is always heartwarming to have them come back to us. Guests often tell us that it was like coming back to their "Miami home".

The Bed and Breakfast has provided a great platform to us as professionals as well as for our community. We enjoy community evolvement and want to be known as a safe place to learn and celebrate Black culture for generations to come. We often host events and have created a space for everything from panel discussions to a free rotating, art gallery. While the stay is cultural, the home of the concept is historical. Breakfast is the most special experience at The Copper Door B&B. The locals in Miami would always ask how they could get the breakfast without staying at the Copper Door B&B, and the answer was that you had to be a guest in order to partake of the breakfast. At the time, breakfast was exclusive to guests only, and there was not an opportunity for locals to indulge unless they became a guest at the Copper Door B&B.

THE BIRTH OF ROSIE'S

Little did we know that the COVID-19 global pandemic, would have other plans for us. Over a very casual conversation with our legal team, a brainstorming session about what to do about COVID led to a suggestion of selling our breakfast to the public since it was so popular. Not much long after, our pop-up restaurant concept, Rosie's was born. We steered the concept as a pivot to generate an alternative means of revenue. At first, there was hardly any traffic: one order, two orders, sometimes no orders. Although, just like we've done in the past, we held strong and stayed true to our vision. We relied on our culinary talents and after a challenging six months, word got out that we had the best breakfast in town.

The Copper Door had an area adjacent to the entrance that was once used as a carport but was vacant since opening. We used the carport as a terminal for guests and delivery drivers to pick up their orders through a window. Rosie's started out as a to-go concept with a limited but delicious menu that was constructed to fit guests and our team's needs amongst a pandemic. A safe pivot was a priority to us before generating revenue. We created the menu based on the idea of comfort food during an uncomfortable time. We focused on feel good food. The initial menu included what today would be considered Rosie's staples: hot crispy chicken, house-made buttermilk biscuits, vanilla-spiced waffles, and Southern polenta. We took the opportunity to take a step back and create the concept with a goal to pay homage to those who had paved the way for us. We named the concept after Jamila's mother's childhood nickname, Rosie. Both of our mothers have individually been strong supporters of our goals as individuals, as well as, as a couple. They have both been a great inspiration to our success. My mother, Katrina West, actually wrote the restaurant's logo and many of the recipes I have developed are originally hers or my grandmother's home recipes.

As the crisis in America escalated throughout the summer months of 2020 and Black Lives Matter became more of a priority across the country, there was an influx of new opportunities that a short six-months prior wasn't available to small businesses and especially not exclusively to small, Black-owned businesses. Jamila always led our efforts when it came to administrative and funding responsibilities, so she made an effort to pursue any and every grant that we qualified for. Through her efforts, we were awarded a Black-owned restaurant grant subsidized through Discover Card, along with a $10,000 grant from the BeyGood Foundation, a collaborative between Beyonce Knowles-Carter and the NAACP. We were able to utilize the funds towards renovating the carport space to create a full-service version of Rosie's. We embellished the space with fresh greenery, ventilation, tables and chairs. With the additional funding, we were also able to hire locals for new positions and train a motivated group of young people who often reminded Jamila and I of ourselves growing up as young adults in the restaurant industry. We have always made our neighborhood and those in need, a priority. During the pandemic, we organized a team specifically to work with food service organizations and other not-for-profit organizations to provide meals with a very simple mission: to provide delicious food for whoever may need it. The humble donations have led to other opportunities with organizations to provide free meals to the community.

Almost immediately, guest reviews started to roll in with 5-star reviews. Regular guests became more regular and we continued to push the envelope to create better food and a more intentional guest experience. Both concepts have been featured in Forbes, Vogue.com, Aventura Magazine, along with many other local publications over the past year. We were awarded the national Starchef Award, as well as the Starchef Community Award in April, 2021. We currently operate both, Rosie's and The Copper Door B&B. Occupancy rates are steadily increasing since the pandemic and we are in search of a more permanent home when it comes to Rosie's.

ADVICE TO ASPIRING ENTREPRENEURS

We encourage those who are interested in entrepreneurship to stay focused, be dedicated to the vision and to keep in mind that the journey is all about baby steps. Create a strong foundation within the field you are interested in mastering, create a solution-based business model that is unique and reach out for help, whether it be mentorship or simply asking someone for professional advice. The road is long and certainly bumpy, but the key is to not give up, but to create solutions and move a bit differently.

AUTHOR'S INFORMATION PAGE

Akino & Jamila West
Rosie's
The Copper Door B&B
439 NW 4th Ave,
Miami, FL 33128
305- 454-9065
www.rosiesmia.com
www.copperdoorbnb.com

Ann Marie Sorrell
The Mosaic Group
West Palm Beach Office
5840 Corporate Way, Ste. 250
West Palm Beach, FL 33407
561-651-9565
www.mosaicgroup.co

Ann McNeill
MCO Construction
6600 NW 27th Ave,
Suite 208
Miami, FL 33147
305-693-4344
www.mcoconstruction.net

Dr. Barbara Sharief
South Florida Pediatric Home Care
3351 N. University Drive
Hollywood, Florida 33024
phone: 954-967-1900
www.southfloridapediatrics.com/

Brenda Riggins
Mars Contractors Inc.
13303 SW 135th Avenue
Miami, FL 33186
(305) 278-2122
www. marscontractors.com

Burnadette Norris -Weeks, Esq.
Partner, Austin-Pamies, Norris-Weeks,
Powell, PLLC
401 North NW 7th Avenue
Fort Lauderdale, Florida 33311
954-768-9770
www.apnwplaw.com/attorneys

Ericka J
801 Pooler Parkway
Pooler, GA 31322
www.hairbyerickaj.com

Dr. Nikki Hyppolite
www.apejewels.com
954-812-3843

Lakitsia Gaines
6704 SW 80th Street
Miami, FL 33143
305-661-4213

1920 E Hallandale Beach Blvd Ph 1
Hallandale Beach, FL 33009
www.kitsiagaines.com

Lanetta Bronte-Hall, M.D.
1685 S. State Road 7
Unit 4
Hollywood, FL
33023
954-397-3251
www.fscdr.org/team/lanetta-bronte-hall

Lisa Ivory
The Ivory Group
18459 Pines Blvd. Suite 473
Pembroke, Pines, FL 33029
954-815-0944

Michelle Swaby
PO Box 260695
Pembroke Pines, FL 33026
954-558-9664
www.pgpppromotions.com

Thema Campbell
Girl Power Rocks, Inc.
1600 NW 3rd Ave
#100
Miami, FL 33136
www.girlpowerrocks.org

Dr. Venessa Walker
Walker Chiropractic & Wellness Center
8844 Miramar Pkwy
Miramar, FL 33025
954- 639-7257
www.walkerchiropracticfl.com

Wendell Locke, Esq.
Locke Law, P.A.
8201 Peters Rd
#1000
Plantation, FL 33324
(954) 382-8858
www.lockefirm.com/attorney/wendell_t_locke

Mia Merritt, Ed. D
Editor & Organizer of this book
Merritt Consulting, Inc.
PO Box 3938
Pembroke Pines, FL
33024
800-669-3604
www.miamerritt.com